WINNING
BALANCE

WINNING
BALANCE

Shawn Johnson

WITH NANCY FRENCH

What I've learned so far
about love, faith,
and living your dreams

**Outstanding
Teen Reader**

Alaina

First Name

ANOKA
COUNTY
LIBRARY

TYNDALE
MOMENTUM

An imprint of
Tyndale House Publishers, Inc.

Visit Tyndale online at www.tyndale.com.

Visit Tyndale Momentum online at www.tyndalemomentum.com.

Visit Shawn online at www.shawnjohnson.net.

TYNDALE and Tyndale's quill logo are registered trademarks of Tyndale House Publishers, Inc.

Tyndale Momentum and the Tyndale Momentum logo are trademarks of Tyndale House Publishers, Inc. Tyndale Momentum is an imprint of Tyndale House Publishers, Inc.

Designed by Beth Sparkman

Edited by Kimberly Miller

Published in association with the literary agency of Shade Global, 10 East 40th Street, 48th Floor, New York, NY 10016.

Library of Congress Cataloging-in-Publication Data

Johnson, Shawn, 1992-
    Winning balance : what I've learned so far about love, faith, and living your dreams / Shawn Johnson ; with Nancy French.
        p. cm.
    Includes bibliographical references.
    ISBN 978-1-4143-7210-5
    1. Athletes—Religious life. 2. Johnson, Shawn, 1992- 3. Athletes—United States—Biography.
4. Gymnasts—United States—Biography. I. French, Nancy, 1974- II. Title.
    BV4596.A8J66 2012
    277.3'083092--dc23
    [B]   2012007978

Printed in the United States of America

18	17	16	15	14	13	12
7	6	5	4	3	2	1

Dedication

To my parents, for never leaving my side.

You have always believed in me, supported me, picked me up, and brought me back down to earth when I needed it. You have given me the opportunity to see my dreams come true, and that is the greatest gift of all.

I know we have had our share of hard times, but through everything, you have given me the world, and I couldn't be more grateful.

I love you . . . "to the moon and back."

Contents

A Note from Shawn *ix*

"My Lord's Prayer" *xi*

Introduction *xiii*

Part 1   **Finding Fire** *1*

CHAPTER 1   Unbreakable *3*

CHAPTER 2   Finding My Place *9*

CHAPTER 3   Just a Normal Girl *21*

CHAPTER 4   Inspiration *29*

CHAPTER 5   The Secret Video *35*

CHAPTER 6   Not Your Average Summer Camp *41*

CHAPTER 7   "Who Is *That* Girl?" *47*

CHAPTER 8   Watch Me, World! *55*

CHAPTER 9   A Cast and Some Power Tools *63*

CHAPTER 10   Travails and Trials *71*

CHAPTER 11   Nothing Is Certain *79*

Part 2   **Champion** *83*

CHAPTER 12   Handstands at 35,000 Feet *85*

CHAPTER 13   The Showdown *93*

CHAPTER 14   The Day I Grew Up *99*

CHAPTER 15   Do Not Make Bob Costas Angry *107*

CHAPTER 16   A Truly Winning Balance *113*

CHAPTER 17   More Than I'd Bargained For *123*

CHAPTER 18   Last Night in Beijing *133*

CHAPTER 19 Proud to Be an American *139*
CHAPTER 20 The Best of Both Worlds *147*

Part 3 Dancing through Life *151*
CHAPTER 21 Hollywood, Here I Come! *153*
CHAPTER 22 Finding My Space *161*
CHAPTER 23 An Arresting Development *167*
CHAPTER 24 Little Bullets *177*
CHAPTER 25 The Mirror Ball of Glory *185*
CHAPTER 26 Learning to Be Me Again *193*
CHAPTER 27 Shaping Up *199*
CHAPTER 28 How God Became More Real to Me *203*
CHAPTER 29 Wipeout *211*

Part 4 Coming Back *217*
CHAPTER 30 Everything Changes *219*
CHAPTER 31 The Surprise Announcement *225*
CHAPTER 32 A New Identity *231*
CHAPTER 33 Just Believe *237*
CHAPTER 34 No Regrets *241*

"My Heart" *247*
Acknowledgments *249*
Endnotes *252*
About the Author *253*

A Note from Shawn

We live by believing and not by seeing.
—2 Corinthians 5:7

OVER THE PAST FIVE YEARS, many articles have been written about me. Most journalists have gotten the details right, though only a few seem to have truly captured something about who I am as a person, not simply as a gymnast. That's understandable, since most reporters have been assigned to cover a specific event or to give readers a status report on my training.

I wrote *Winning Balance* as a way to go deeper. Though my story is presented chronologically, it is not my autobiography. Instead, I wrote this book as a way to reflect on the lessons I've learned during nearly two decades of training, competition, and most important, everyday life.

That's why I chose to end almost every chapter with a short reflection called "Lesson I've Learned." Each one summarizes a key principle I've gained from my family, my sport, or my faith. I hope these lessons, along with my poems throughout the book, will inspire you as you seek to live your dreams as well. Even though your passions and background may be quite different from mine, I believe there is much we can teach each other.

Perhaps the greatest lessons I've learned so far are these: Everything happens for a reason, and God can be trusted to work all things together for good. I don't know what lies ahead for me, but I am convinced that I am on the right road. My hope is that something I've learned will help you, too, even if you can't see what's coming or if life's pathway has gotten a bit bumpy.

May we all enjoy the adventure that comes when we walk together—by faith.

Shawn Johnson

FEBRUARY 2012

MY LORD'S PRAYER

Now I lay me down to sleep.
My heart is yours to find, to seek.
You keep me safe and hold me tight,
Helping me decide what's right.
You watch me fall but help me up,
Never wanting to disrupt
Life's set path to which I face.
Destiny has its own set pace.
You give me wings and help me fly,
But always keep your distance—why?
Why is it you hide in us,
Causing us to find your trust?
You surround me in the waves of light,
But others find it hard to fight
The passion with reality,
Never letting their minds just be
Natural in believing in you,
Instead of feeling like the countless few.
We feel your warmth within our hearts,
Relying on that so we don't fall apart,
Relying on love to keep us intact
So we can move on and never look back.
I love you for who you've grown to be
Or who it is I've grown to see.
I pray to you to watch me close.
Have faith in me; don't let me boast.

Watch my family and my friends;
Guide them in helping their hearts to mend.
Watch them sleep throughout the nights;
Stay by their side with all your light.
I pray you see our hearts' true beat.
I pray the Lord my soul to keep.

Introduction

Olympics

August 2008

Beijing

THIS WAS IT—THE MOMENT I had worked for with all my might every day for almost as long as I could remember.

I was standing in the 2008 Olympic arena in Beijing with eighteen thousand people in the stands and hundreds of millions watching across the globe. My friend and teammate Nastia Liukin was preparing to begin her floor exercise and final rotation for the women's individual all-around competition. I would follow her, and I knew I had to give the floor routine of my life.

I'd set my sights on the highest possible goal—Olympic gold. The women's all-around is the most prestigious gymnastics event at the Olympics, the biggest prize of all. It was also the goal I'd had my eyes on since I knew that the Olympics were even a remote possibility. I was competing with twenty-three of the world's best female gymnasts, who represented fifteen different countries. Just a few days before, I'd taken the top spot in the preliminaries, when ninety-eight gymnasts had been vying for a spot in the finals.

To win the gold in this all-around competition, a gymnast has to get high scores in the vault, the uneven bars, the balance beam, and the floor exercise. It's called "all-around" because each of the four events showcases important—and different—gymnastics skills. The vault shows strength, the uneven bars display agility, the beam

proves the ability to concentrate under pressure, and the floor exercise demonstrates showmanship. Most gymnasts excel in just one of
these disciplines, but the best all-around is someone who excels in
all of them. In the Olympics, there would be no higher honor than
winning a gold right here, right now.

I had arrived at the Olympics as the reigning world champion,
having won the all-around in Germany the year before, when I
was fifteen. Then, back in June, I'd won the women's Visa National
Championships and two weeks later the Olympic Trials. In one sense,
these victories seemed to put me in position to take the Olympic
gold. However, winners of the world title are rarely able to follow up
with an Olympic gold in the all-around. Gymnastics, after all, is the
most fickle of sports. So many factors go into whether a performance
is medal-worthy—injuries, emotional distractions, rest, diet, the
judges' preferences, and even crowd reaction. With victory depending
on so many variables, the competitions are exciting; the results, often
unexpected. No one is ever guaranteed a win.

Mary Lou Retton won this competition in 1984, and I'd been
compared to her throughout the Beijing Games. There was something about my muscular energy—as opposed to the artistry of
the petite, pixie-like gymnasts—that caused viewers to make the
comparison. To add to the pressure, I knew that somewhere up in
the stands Mary Lou was watching . . . and hoping I would nail
this routine.

I'd been told a thousand times since we'd landed in China that
"this was my moment." All of the missed leisure time, school hours,
and dates had allowed me to focus on preparing for this competition, including the floor routine that was just seconds away.

Thankfully, the United States, represented by Nastia and me in
the all-around, was in good shape. We had both done well on bars
and vault. Not long before I had given a clean performance on the
beam, sticking my dismount to enthusiastic applause.

Looking ahead to the floor competition, I was confident that if I hit my routine, I could win the gold. The floor exercise was one of my strongest events, and I could barely wait to get out there, where I could conceivably go all the way.

Then I broke one of my rules. My coaches had taught me from day one not to distract myself by watching the scoreboard at competitions. But this day of all days, I had a strong urge to look at it. When I glanced up, I nearly lost my breath. Scanning the top names, I noticed that mine was not among them. In fact, I was all the way down in eighth place.

What had gone wrong? I'd been competing at an international level for several years, and I'd never been so low—even after falling off a beam!

I've always loved math. Not only can I easily figure out how much to tip a good server at a restaurant or how much money I could save by getting the jeans on the sale rack, I can also quickly calculate what scores gymnasts need to receive in order to advance.

Looking at everybody's scores after the beam competition, I did a quick calculation. I knew who still had to go up in scoring and what scores they had to get. I also knew what score I had to get to receive a gold medal.

I tried to push these numbers out of my mind as we warmed up on the floor. After the Chinese and Russian gymnasts had given strong performances, Nastia competed with the seamless elegance she's known for. Now I was waiting on the blue mat, ready to show the world what I could do. As soon as Nastia's score was announced, I would be given the signal to go and would have my chance at the top spot on the podium.

When her score flashed on the screen, my stomach dropped.

15.525. That gave her a final overall score of 63.325—a full seven-tenths of a point higher than the highest possibility I'd calculated while standing on the sidelines.

On TV, the announcers were telling the world what my quick calculations had already told me. I would not win the gold medal. Even if I went out on the mat and performed perfectly, my score wouldn't be high enough to capture the gold.

My ultimate dream was out of reach.

PART I

Finding Fire

Find the fire deep inside.
Watch it burn and stay alive.
Keep it lit and give it a light.
Give it life and make it bright.
Know that what you do is who you are:
Forever and always you'll be a star.

CHAPTER I

UNBREAKABLE

Other things may change us, but we start and end with family.
—*Anthony Brandt*

THE FIRST SCORE I EVER received was given on January 19, 1992, at Iowa Lutheran Hospital in Des Moines. I was one minute old when the doctor took me aside to perform the routine Apgar test, a simple examination given to newborns to determine their health at birth. The Apgar—which stands for appearance, pulse, grimace, activity, and respiration—evaluates the baby's muscle tone, heart rate, facial movement, reflexes, and breathing. Based on those factors, the test assigns a score from zero to ten.

After taking medication to prevent premature labor, my mom had anxiously waited for her due date—and then waited some more. Despite fears that I would arrive early, I actually arrived late. When the doctor discovered the umbilical cord was wrapped around my neck, he called a neonatal specialist to work on me as soon as I was born. My parents could tell something was wrong by the concerned look on the doctor's face and the frantic way the nurses were caring for me.

They watched as the specialist worked on me in the corner of the room before telling my parents that they needed to move me to the neonatal nursery. Dad followed the nurses when they whisked me away. He wasn't going to let me out of his sight. And I wasn't looking good. The first thing Dad noticed was that my skin looked gray. The doctor said I had been without oxygen for a while, so I wasn't responding the way a healthy baby should. They put me in an incubator for forty-eight hours so they could monitor my health, and I became more responsive pretty quickly.

Only later, when my parents were going through paperwork, did they see the score of my Apgar test: a big, fat zero.

By that time, though, I'd recovered from my trauma and looked like any other healthy six-pound, nine-ounce newborn. My parents were hoping I'd be strong enough to one day run and play like other kids, but they had no idea that the nearly seven-pound bundle of joy they were holding was a future Olympic champion.

After all, even if I'd had an easy birth, there was no reason to believe I'd be particularly athletic. Dad played hockey and wrestled in school, but Mom never participated in organized sports. She did gymnastics recreationally but never competed. However, both Mom and Dad roller-skated, which is what brought them together. They met when they were only thirteen years old at a roller rink in a small Iowa town. Maybe it was the romantic music playing over the loudspeaker or maybe it was just destiny, but soon they were skating hand in hand around that rink.

They saw each other around town whenever possible, even though they didn't attend the same school. Because her family moved several times, Mom attended three different high schools in the area. Yet Dad was a constant in her life. Mom had a little motorbike, which she would ride four miles to see him. They also sat together at football games, and Mom started going to Dad's wrestling matches. In 1977, they decided to get married two weeks after Mom graduated from high school. Because she was just seventeen, she had to get her parents' permission. Needless to say, their engagement raised eyebrows around town. The fact that I didn't show up until fifteen years later quieted the rumors.

In the meantime, Dad went to work for a construction company, learning to frame and then becoming especially skilled at interior trim work. Several years before I was born, he and his brother started their own contracting business. Mom, who had grown up helping her mom keep the records for her stepdad's business, continued working in bookkeeping and accounting.

Growing up, Mom's family had moved around a lot, so once she was married, she worked hard to create a warm, welcoming home with my dad. Not long after they married, they got a dog, the first of several family pets. Dude, their first golden retriever, arrived just about a year before I did. He would become one of my first playmates.

Once Mom was pregnant, they talked about choosing the perfect name. They loved "Shawn," which was going to be my name whether I was a girl or a boy. If I'd been a boy, I would have been Shaun Douglas, after my dad. However, since I was a girl, I was named Shawn Machel (pronounced like the traditional spelling "Michelle") after my mother, Teri Machel Johnson. I used to hate my name because the kids at school thought it was a boy's name. However, I've grown to love its strength, uniqueness, and meaning: God is gracious.

By the time we left the hospital, my parents had the healthy newborn they'd waited so long for. Though they were certainly ready to welcome a baby, Mom was a little afraid. I seemed so delicate and tiny. When she gave me a bath, she was more hesitant than if she had been washing fine china. When she changed my diaper, she was worried she'd hurt me.

That's how Dad ended up doing a lot of the bathing and the feeding when we first came home from the hospital. After working all day doing trim work, he would come home and immediately bathe, feed, and take care of me until bedtime. This might explain why I'm such a daddy's girl even to this day.

Once when I was still a baby, I was lying on the couch when Dude, who had just noticed movement outside the window, jumped on top of me to get a closer look. Mom was convinced that I'd punctured my lungs and frantically called the doctor.

"Well," he asked, "is she breathing?"

"Yes," my mom replied.

"Then," he assured her, "she's going to be just fine."

After a few months, Mom learned I wasn't nearly as breakable as she thought. She found that my arms could actually be raised and bent to fit into my tiny clothes. My head survived, even when she stretched the opening of a shirt to fit around it. Bathing me and changing my diaper now came naturally . . . no matter how much I wriggled.

And—wow—did I wriggle.

In fact, by the time I was about six months old, my mom began noticing that when I eyed something, I was so determined to get it that I rolled sideways until I could reach it. I completely skipped the crawling stage. When I was nine months old, my parents looked up one day to see me toddling into their room, grinning from ear to ear. I had flipped out of my crib and sauntered to their bedroom. They had no idea how I'd learned to walk.

I never slowed down after that. Once, I crawled up on the kitchen counter to try skydiving. (Hey, I was little . . . so the counter seemed as high as the sky to me back then.) When I landed, my teeth went through my bottom lip, and there was blood everywhere. But that injury didn't stop me for long. As a toddler, I would pile all of my toys on the floor as a makeshift ladder to reach the top of our entertainment center. From there, I'd jump onto the red leather couch, pretending it was a trampoline.

Even more fun than trying these daredevil tricks myself was urging my cousin, Tori, to do them with me. Tori, the daughter of my mom's sister, is two years older than I am and a bit more cautious. I had to talk her into doing flips over our couch. When she stayed over on Saturday nights, we'd sleep in the bunk beds in our basement. I loved to do flips and pull-ups on them, as well as hang from the bars. At first Tori just watched, but before long she was doing them with me.

Tori and I also loved to play outdoors. Sometimes we dressed up and acted out stories; other times we would take turns tying a rope around our waists and pulling each other in a wagon. Since I was smaller and younger than Tori, I'd also jump on her back and let her carry me around.

I'm an only child and Tori's brother is eight years older, so I guess it's not surprising that we not only played like sisters—we also fought like them. I admit I was usually the instigator. When we'd be playing in the basement, occasionally I'd hit her lightly, waiting for her to respond. Almost always, she'd give me a funny look and keep playing. But I'd go running upstairs, crying that Tori had hit me. Though she was the one who got in trouble, she never held it against me.

Tori also joined me in my first tumbling and dancing classes. Because I was so physically active, Mom decided she needed to find an outlet for all of my energy. Even though Tori went with me, I had no desire to continue either of those activities. So my mom took me to a local gymnastics center and signed me up. It's not that she was particularly fond of the sport. She just knew that I needed a large, open (and soft!) place to play. And I loved it. Even though the coaches were very strict, I enjoyed tumbling and running and always had a smile on my face while I was there. For three years,

I happily went to the gym at least once a week. My coach told my
mom that I was full of energy, but not full of talent.

Then Mom heard about a new gym that was closer to our home.
One day after dropping me off at my gymnastics class, Mom drove to
that facility and watched a class through the windows. She was struck
by how happy all the young gymnasts appeared and how much fun
they seemed to be having. She never imagined that she was staring at
my future.

Lesson I've Learned

Even if you fly high in life, stay grounded. From
the time I was very small, my parents supported my
daring ventures out into the world, while making
home a place I always wanted to come back to.

CHAPTER 2

FINDING MY PLACE

Be who you are and say what you feel because those who
mind don't matter and those who matter don't mind.

—*Dr. Seuss*

A FEW DAYS LATER, my mom walked me into Chow's Gymnastics
and Dance Institute for the first time. On one side of the large
gym, an Asian man was setting up equipment. My mom stopped to
talk to the woman in the office, who we later learned was the man's
wife. While my mom asked her about classes, I spotted the uneven
bars and ran over to them. I began swinging on them right away,
flashing my baby-toothed grin toward the man.

That man, who would soon become my coach, was named Qiao
Liang, but he told us that day that he'd prefer if we called him simply
Chow. Eight years before, his exceptional career with the Chinese
national gymnastics team had ended, and twenty-three-year-old
Chow had to decide what to do next. With images of the New York
skyline in mind, he decided to move from Beijing to coach at the
University of Iowa. No sooner had he landed on a snowy airstrip in
January—with no skyline or even trees in sight—than his new boss,

9

Iowa gymnastics coach Tom Dunn, met him and drove him to the gym at the university. Tom told him to begin coaching the male gymnasts who'd arrived for practice—despite the fact that Chow had just completed a thirteen-plus-hour flight from China and was still wearing the dress clothes he'd traveled in.

That was not the only shock that awaited him. As an elite gymnast in China, Chow had never had to cook or clean for himself—his daily needs were met so he could focus completely on gymnastics. Now, after years of enjoying the perks and fame of an elite athlete in China, he was suddenly a poor college student in Iowa. He rose at five o'clock each morning to prepare for his English classes at the university. After classes ended in the early afternoon, he coached the gymnasts until early evening. Then Chow headed home to prepare and eat dinner before starting on homework that often wasn't done until one or two in the morning. After a few hours of sleep, he began the process all over again. Despite the culture shock and challenges in communicating with his athletes, five of Chow's gymnasts qualified for the national team in his first year. As he coached them to become better athletes, they helped him learn English faster.

Within a year, Chow was able to focus solely on gymnastics and began coaching Iowa's women's team. Not long after, he married his former teammate from the Beijing city team, Liwen Zhaung—or Li, as I call her.

Chow and Li dreamed of coaching national and world champions, but after seven years at the university, they realized that in order to make that happen, they needed to train and develop gymnasts from a very early age. So they followed their own American dream and opened Chow's Gymnastics and Dance Institute.

Within a week of my first visit, I was enrolled at the new gym and hanging on the uneven bars like a monkey. Though I was fearless and comfortable on the equipment, Chow recommended to my mom that I be moved back a few levels so I could relearn some of the fundamentals properly. Though my mom was surprised, she didn't resist. In fact, she laid down just one ground rule: "I will never make her come here," she told Chow. "I just won't. This is supposed to be fun, and we'll stay here only as long as it's fun."

Thankfully, Chow made it fun. He never told my parents I'd be any sort of world champion. Instead, he told them I had a lot of potential. Other gymnasts at the elite level—particularly in Chow's home country of China—often train as much as many American adults work per week. In fact, Chow himself was chosen at a very young age to become a champion. At only ten years old, he had left his home and moved to a school specializing in gymnastics.

Maybe that's why his philosophy regarding children in the sport was so refreshingly different from many ambitious and successful coaches. He always claimed that no coach can look at a kid when she is six and determine whether she'll be a champion.

"You're supposed to have a real life," he'd say. "And to have fun." That may explain why the atmosphere in his gym was so different from the first place where I had trained. At my original gym, we weren't allowed to fidget. But Chow would let me go off and do cartwheels and flips while waiting in line.

"Don't let her get away with that kind of thing," Mom said one day after arriving early to pick me up and seeing my antics. "She can stand in line like everyone else!"

"I don't mind her being a kid," he assured her. He never minded my playfulness because he knew it wasn't the result of a lack of discipline. Instead, he saw my high energy as evidence of my desire to better myself, to get on the equipment where the work was done. In fact, he considered my desire to be in motion a benefit, and he focused on teaching me how to concentrate when it *really* mattered. At the same time, he made sure that I—and all his gymnasts—had plenty of space and time to master new skills.

While gymnastics was becoming a larger part of my life, my

parents were determined that I would have the normal childhood they wanted for me. I attended Westridge Elementary, located near the two interstates that connect West Des Moines to the rest of the country. When I began attending kindergarten there, it was immediately clear that I loved school and learning. I was always the teacher's pet. My instructors would frequently ask me to help them outside of the classroom. I loved doing schoolwork because I liked to figure things out. My insatiable curiosity led me to read my textbooks like they contained the secrets to life. I was an interesting combination of nerd, tomboy, and girlie girl . . . which, come to think of it, is probably still a good description.

In the evenings, Mom would take me to gymnastics and watch from the viewing area with the other parents. Even though I'd only started gymnastics because it was a fun and safe place to play, I ended up enjoying it so much that I went several times per week. The more I enjoyed the sport, the more I went to the gym. The more I practiced, the more maneuvers I could do. The more skills I developed, the more fun I had.

"I made the pre-team!" I told my mom excitedly one day when I was six years old. Unlike toddlers in ballet class, who usually end up in a recital wearing ballet slippers and tutus, kids in gymnastics class do not necessarily get to perform publicly. Competitions are a privilege earned through work, even at a young age. Chow evaluated his recreational gymnasts and hand-selected a group of us to be on the "pre-team," which was an easy place to begin learning competitive skills. I loved to learn the new routines, though I never considered it "work." At that stage of life, everything was fun and games. Over the course of the year, I got better and stronger. And when I was seven, I made the team.

Gymnasts at this point are divided into levels, beginning at 1 and going to 10. Once I mastered a certain skill set, I'd move up another level. When I was seven, I was at level 5, which was the first level at which Chow allowed gymnasts to take part in competitions. By this point I practiced about nine hours a week, mostly in the evenings when Mom came home from work.

My first gymnastics meet was in Iowa City at the university. I wasn't nervous at all. When I was waiting to begin my routine, I stood on one side of the beam and the judges stood on the other. Because I was so tiny, I couldn't see over the top of the beam, so I kept popping up on my tiptoes to see if the judges had signaled me to begin. Though my scores were not memorable, I still remember seeing my mom and dad beaming at me from the audience, along with hundreds of other smiling faces.

Even the judges laughed at the sight of this tiny, leotard-wearing kid bouncing up and down. Between rotations, they played songs during warm-ups. I danced while I waited, without a care in the world. When it came time to get ribbons, I actually got one—the worse you did, the more colorful the ribbon. So, I took my pretty ribbon and was absolutely thrilled.

Level 5 introduced me to the joy of competition, yet it also very well might have been the end of my gymnastics "career." I had begun gymnastics with great enthusiasm and progressed rapidly for several years. However, even though the judges might have thought I was a cute—if short and slightly pudgy-looking—gymnast, they didn't score me very high.

In fact, when the season ended, my mom told Coach Chow that she and my dad would be perfectly happy if he decided to keep me at level 5 for another year. Yet this time Chow recommended moving me up. That's because he and Li knew something my parents didn't: the skill set at level 5 worked to the advantage of tall, lean gymnasts. But the coaches knew that mastering the skill set for level 6 would require physical power—a strength of mine even then.

Because of my body type and my frequent workouts at the gym, my muscles were developing faster than those of other kids my age.

Given that I was a short kid with huge biceps, six-pack abs, and the name Shawn, my classmates weren't always sure what to think of me. The boys didn't like me because they—rightly—figured that I could beat them up. And many of the girls didn't like me because I looked like a boy and had a boy's name. I definitely wanted to fit in, but over the course of my months at the gym I'd gotten a little competitive, even outside of my sport.

"I'm going to win so many awards!" I told my dad one day when I got home from school. Field day was coming up, and I could hardly wait. I'd signed up for all kinds of activities because it was my favorite day of the year.

"Really?" he asked. "What are you doing?"

"The one-hundred-yard dash, potato-sack race, softball throw, and pull-ups," I read from the list I'd brought home. Then I asked him, "Dad, what's a softball?"

Within the hour, Dad had driven to the store, bought me a softball, and begun throwing balls to me in the backyard. I can't remember if I won the softball throw that year, but I definitely won the pull-up competition. My main rival was a little boy who valiantly pulled his chin over the bar with much effort. I'd been doing this at Chow's every day, so I knew I was going to dominate in that contest. I carefully counted to see how many he struggled to get—nine. So I went up and did ten, without even breaking a sweat. That way I won the contest but didn't show off the fact that I could've done pull-ups until the end of the school day.

I had two simultaneous, frequently conflicting desires. I wanted to win, and I wanted to be just like everyone else. I didn't want my strength to artificially separate me from my peers. But I found the cliques at school to be impenetrable. So I did cartwheels on the playground while the other girls ran around in groups and were chased by boys who apparently had a bad infestation of the cooties.

Once a girl in my class came up to me.

"Want to be in our group and run around with us on the playground?"

"Sure," I said, trying to hide my excitement.

"Well, we have to vote."

By the end of the day—apparently without much deliberation—I got the bad news.

"Sorry," she said, though I didn't think she meant it. "We voted, and they said no."

I was always the girl who didn't fit well into any neat, prepackaged friend group. At school I was quiet, kept to myself, got my work done, and left. But at the gym, I fit in effortlessly. There was something equalizing about wearing those leotards. In school, we always had the popularity contest about who wore what clothing. But at Chow's, it was so easy. All I had to do was throw on a leotard and put my hair in a ponytail, and suddenly I looked just like all the other girls in the gym. It wasn't about who was wearing the coolest clothes; it was all about the sport. Those girls at Chow's were like my sisters. Though we came from different schools, and even different towns, they were my constant support system.

We lived in West Des Moines, Iowa, which is a suburb of our state's capital city. Though our state is known for all the politicking that goes on here, my family never really paid attention to the politicians who showed up every four years. To us Des Moines was the "insurance capital of the world," because for some reason our city has attracted a huge insurance industry. America's heartland is a wonderful place to grow up. The people are incredibly friendly and pull together in good times and bad. West Des Moines will always feel like home to me.

My family has lived in the same house at the end of a cul-de-sac in a quiet little neighborhood since I was six. We had friendly neighbors, a good backyard, a big tree that I loved to climb, and railroad tracks that provided the perfect soundtrack for childhood.

When the train passed during the day, it was so common I didn't really notice it. But at night, as I lay in bed, I'd hear it slowly churning by, blasting a warning whistle as it passed through the town. For me, it was comforting. Some of our neighbors didn't like the sound, but to me it defined childhood as much as carrying my lunch box to school or playing with my dad in the cul-de-sac.

I was always Dad's little sidekick, and as I got older, he taught me things that most girls my age never learned. Plus, we would spend hours and hours fishing. I loved being outside, but some things did make me squeamish. Mostly, I had an intense fear of bugs. I hated them, I didn't want to see them, and I'd sometimes slightly overreact when I saw them. Okay, I'd freak out. But Dad was always there to take care of the creepy crawlies, and I appreciated him for that.

Though we had a peaceful life, I tried my best to spice it up. I'm an adrenaline junkie . . . a trait I must've inherited from my dad. He played hockey, raced cars, and loved to have adventures. Like him, I tried to get an adrenaline rush out of anything when I was a kid. There was a house at the top of the hill before the turn onto our street, and my friends and I used to take skateboards up there. All five of us would line up in a row, sit on our skateboards, and use our hands to push ourselves as fast as we could down the street. Of course, we wanted to see who could make it to the end without wiping out halfway down.

Though my parents tolerated my daredevil antics and wholeheartedly supported my passion for gymnastics, they always made it clear that they were most concerned about the way I treated other people. In elementary school, one of my classmates was a brilliant kid with limited social skills. On top of that, he was big for his age. When kids made fun of him, he would suddenly explode in anger. Maybe because I often felt misunderstood by my peers, I felt sorry for him. When I noticed he always sat alone on the bus, I began sitting next to him.

My mom was friendly to him as well, and we sometimes talked about how hurtful kids can act toward those who seem different. My mom reminded me over and over that there is never any reason to hurt someone else's feelings. We are to "do unto others as we would have them do unto us," she said. She also told me that though I can't prevent people from telling lies about me, I can choose to live in such a way that their words never become reality. My character is completely within my control.

I learned another powerful lesson in second or third grade when my mom picked me up after school with a serious look on her face. I was already squirming a bit when she turned to face me. She told me that she'd gotten a call from my teacher, who had caught me cheating on a test. I was so ashamed that I wanted the ground to swallow me up.

As I began crying, my mom didn't lecture me. Instead, she asked me how I had felt inside when I cheated. I said I felt bad. She told me that bad feeling was a voice in my heart telling me that what I was doing was wrong. "If you don't want to feel that way again," she said, "you need to listen to that voice." Little more was said about it, but I've tried to pay attention to those inner promptings ever since.

Through their quiet example and daily instruction, my parents taught me traditional values like kindness, honesty, and the importance of hard work. Yet in other ways I had a nontraditional upbringing. Take my spiritual life, for example. Both of my parents had a strong faith and wanted the same for me, but for a variety of reasons we didn't regularly attend church like many of our neighbors and friends did.

Dad grew up going to church occasionally. My mom's grandparents were very strong and united in their Christian faith, but my mom grew up with one parent who was Southern Baptist and another who was a Reformed Latter-day Saint. She was turned off by all the arguments over factions and minor points of doctrine, as well as the hypocrisy she saw among some people who called themselves Christians.

Though we were never regular churchgoers, Mom and Dad talked freely with me about God. They taught me to look to him as a tremendous source of comfort and peace through all of life's ups and downs. They encouraged me to talk with him, and I know my mom regularly prayed for me.

My mom even had this prayer, which she knew I liked, painted on the wall of my bedroom:

Now I lay me down to sleep,
I pray the Lord my soul to keep.
See me safely through the night,
And wake me with the morning light.

Mom always encouraged me to say my prayers at night and taught me basic spiritual values, but I didn't get a lot of formal instruction in the facts of the Bible except at Christmas or Easter services or at summer vacation Bible school.

From an early age, I felt drawn to my heavenly Father. Though we didn't go to services except on major holidays, I always felt at home in church. I particularly loved Easter—both the traditions (like the eggs, the bunny, and the little cookies they'd give you at church) and the promise of new life.

We didn't go to church regularly for another reason: since I practiced Monday through Saturday, Sunday was our family day. It was our only day to sleep in, and my mom always cooked breakfast and made a big deal of it. I loved pancakes, which she'd make every morning. On Sundays, however, she'd make me an even bigger stack of pancakes, or would branch out slightly with French toast or waffles. She'd sometimes make eggs, bacon, sausage, or the best homemade "monkey bread." She'd cut biscuits into quarters, roll them in butter, brown sugar, and cinnamon sugar, and then bake the loaf. She would even pour caramel syrup over it, a nice way to top off our Sunday morning breakfast.

I'd frequently eat in my pajamas, since we didn't have to rush off anywhere. Like most kids, I loved watching weekend cartoons—*Tom & Jerry*, *SpongeBob*, and *Rugrats*—which seemed to drive the demands of the gym and school far from my mind. Though we weren't necessarily at church, Sundays were almost sacred days for Mom and Dad, because it was the one day they had their kid back. My parents didn't hate religion; they were simply protective of our time together.

My mom says she realizes now that she had taken her religious instruction for granted because she'd been dragged to church during her childhood and didn't like it. She just assumed that because she knew the names of the twelve apostles, that knowledge would somehow be passed down to me. She realized that wasn't going to happen after an awkward encounter I had in the lunchroom.

"Who's Joseph?" I asked one day in the school cafeteria.

I wanted to participate in the conversation my friends were having about Sunday school, but I didn't have much to contribute. They all looked at me blankly.

"Who's Joseph?" they repeated, in disbelief. "You know, the father of Jesus?" They expected recognition to flash across my face, but still . . . nothing.

That afternoon, when I saw Mom, I told her about the incident.

"I want to go to church," I said.

She looked surprised. "Why don't we go to church?" I persisted, but I knew. Sunday was my only day off from gymnastics.

Mom calmly tried to give me peace of mind. She explained that the other girls shouldn't have been so unkind to me.

"That's not the right way to treat people," she explained. "Just because those girls have more knowledge than you do doesn't mean you are less worthy or important."

Mom wiped away a tear from my cheek. "You can have your own way of dealing with God, and it's okay if you deal with him differently from the other kids."

Though Mom was sensitive to the fact that I wanted to start attending church more regularly, she was never the type of person who let others dictate how she raised me.

So my lunchroom conversation didn't suddenly cause us to start going to Sunday school, and I wouldn't soon be rattling off the books of the Bible. However, both Mom and I learned a lot that day. She learned that religious instruction wasn't passed on to children automatically, and I learned that I really wanted to know more about God. Of course, part of this was because I wanted to be able to participate in the lunchroom conversations with my friends. But I also had a deep desire to understand God's character. Instead of counting sheep, I secretly wondered about him as I lay in bed at night.

As nice as those Easter services were, I knew I wanted more.

Lesson I've Learned

You can work hard and still have fun. You're more likely to stick with something if you find it both challenging and enjoyable. Fortunately, my coaches and parents understood that, and they never had to push me to practice. I found gymnastics so rewarding that I pushed myself.

CHAPTER 3

JUST A NORMAL GIRL

Life is a series of thousands of tiny miracles.
—*Mike Greenberg*

"Shawn, you need to do your homework."

Startled, I looked up to see my math teacher standing over me. "I finished it."

"Well, then," she said with a slight smile, "do tomorrow's assignment."

"I finished that, too."

"You finished tomorrow's homework?" I guess she didn't know what to say next, because she just shook her head and walked away.

What I didn't tell her was that I'd finished my math homework for the entire month. I had a syllabus with the upcoming assignments and had worked ahead. Math came easily to me, but more important, I'd learned early on that I had to be as disciplined about finding time to finish homework as I was about training in the gym.

By second grade, I went to Chow's after school from about 4:30 to 8:30 every weeknight. That meant once I got home from school,

I'd have a quick snack and change into my leotard before my mom drove me to the gym. If I had homework, I had to finish it when I came home in the evening. Because I wanted to do well at both school and gymnastics, I was multitasking before I'd even heard the word.

That didn't mean every day was easy, though. Sometimes I didn't get enough rest, and once in a while I had a meltdown on my way home from practice. Over time, my parents devised a routine to help me cope. When I got home from the gym at the end of a tough day, my dad would make me homemade French toast, using real butter and Wonder bread. It was my absolute favorite. After we ate together, we'd watch TV. I'd sit next to my mom, who'd give me a back rub.

No matter what kind of day I'd had, I could count on Dude running toward me, tail wagging, as soon as I walked in from school or from practice. He expected nothing from me except my companionship. Perhaps that's one reason my family's dogs have always been so important to me.

One day when I was in fourth grade, my dad showed up at school and signed me out. When we were in his truck, he explained that Dude's veterinarian had had to put him to sleep. I knew that Dude had been very sick, but I was crushed. My dad took me out to lunch so we could talk and cry together. Then he let me stay home from school for the rest of the day. Over the next week, the house seemed much too quiet. We all hated coming home without Dude to greet us at the door.

About two weeks later, I walked into my dad's home office and saw him and my mom looking at something on the Internet. It turned out they were searching for a new dog. Worried that I might assume they were trying to replace Dude—something we all knew was impossible—they asked me, "Shawn, how would you feel about adopting another dog?"

A few days later we drove to Nevada, Iowa, a small town just east of Ames. A couple there had recently adopted two puppies and then discovered the wife was pregnant with twins. The thought of raising four "babies" seemed like too much, so they posted an ad on the Internet seeking homes for their two golden retriever puppies. As soon as we walked into their house, one of the puppies caught my eye. Not long after, I carried him in my arms to the car. Tucker has been my baby ever since. When I was younger, I let him chase me as I rode my scooter; once I got my driver's license, I started taking him through the McDonald's drive-through for a small cup of ice cream or to Starbucks for a doggy latte.

Losing Dude was tough, and as my parents knew, it took me a while to sort out my feelings of sadness. I've always been a deep thinker, but I've never been good at sharing my thoughts, opinions, and feelings out loud. I think that's one reason I began writing poetry—it allowed me to make sense of what I was feeling. When I was in second grade, three pieces I wrote were included in an anthology of poetry and short stories written by Iowa schoolchildren. I still remember how proud I was when I got to read them aloud in a local chocolate shop.

When I was in seventh grade, my teacher had us write a poem about ourselves. This was a dream assignment for me, and I took weeks getting the words just right. My classmates, most of whom submitted poems with titles like "A Cool Guy Who Likes Girls," were baffled by my poem, which I called "A Caring Girl Who Loves to Flip." When I read it today, I'm amazed at how my basic outlook on life hasn't changed all that much. The poem ends this way:

I understand that nothing is easy.
I say everything happens for a reason.
I dream of one day the world is in peace.

I try to see the good in everything.
I am a caring girl who loves to flip.

I started writing in a journal in elementary school. That's where I jotted down some of my poetry; it's also where I wrote inspirational quotes. Sometimes while reading I'd come across a sentence that stopped me short and made me think, *That's just how I feel!* Whenever I had that reaction, I jotted down the quote in a journal. I've always loved to draw, too, and my early journals are filled with drawings of hearts and rainbows. Gymnastics required intense focus much of the time; journaling and drawing provided a release and a much-needed break from that, at least briefly.

Looking back, I realize that my parents maintained an incredible balancing act: they supported me wholeheartedly in gymnastics, which I loved, but they also worked hard to keep my life as normal as possible. That meant I went to public school rather than being homeschooled. When I expressed interest in joining the track team with some friends during middle school, my parents encouraged me to go out for it. I had a blast doing the high jump and the long jump and running sprints. Eventually, though, my track coaches wanted me to devote more hours to the sport, which was impossible given my gymnastics schedule. That ended my track career, though not my love of it. I got to be a part of class activities, too, like dancing in my elementary school's production of *100 Years of Broadway.*

My mom and dad knew how to keep me grounded. They recognized my talent and drive for gymnastics, yet they reminded me that everyone is special at something. My mom and I spent a lot of time driving to and from the gym, but we also enjoyed unwinding by scrapbooking and shopping together.

Gymnastics was never my whole life, but it was always my

passion. The gym was like my playground. I loved growing up wearing a leotard. I loved the daily repetition of the movements that reinforced my skills on the balance beam. I loved conditioning every day, with all of my friends neatly in rows, walking, flipping, and stretching our bodies to increase our already improbable flexibility. I loved competing against my friends as well as against myself. I loved what it felt like to finally try out a move on the beam after practicing on a line on the floor for weeks. I loved getting back on the bars after falling. I loved flying through the air.

Practice began with at least thirty minutes to an hour of conditioning, stretching, and endurance training. For strength training, my teammates and I did push-ups, sit-ups, squat jumps, and pull-ups. I then spent about fifty minutes working on each event—balance beam, floor exercise, vault, and uneven bars. Coach Chow trained me in vault, bars, and the tumbling elements of my floor routines. Coach Li worked with me on the balance beam and the dance component of my floor routine. Mats and foam pits under each apparatus allow gymnasts to practice new moves safely. But my coaches also never let me do something they didn't feel I was ready to do without hurting myself.

Every three months, Chow and Li evaluated their students to see whether they were ready to move up to the next level. Gradually but steadily I advanced. Every level of recreational gymnastics requires a new set of skills, each building on the previous ones. Chow and Li had coaching down to an art—they knew exactly how hard to push me. In turn, I wanted to work as hard as I could to become the best that I could be. I was usually the last athlete to leave the gym each evening, simply because I always wanted one more chance to get a skill right.

I was lucky to enroll at Chow's shortly after it opened. That meant I had Coach Chow and Coach Li's full attention from the start. They told me I was talented, but more than that, they affirmed my desire to follow their direction and make even the tiniest corrections.

As former top gymnasts themselves, Chow and Li were masters at the technical side of gymnastics. Equally important, I think, was their ability to train me and their other athletes to prepare mentally for meets. They taught us that competition was just a reflection of our training.

Mistakes, we learned, were normal. After all, we're human. But if we prepared well and put in 100 percent while competing, our chances of making mistakes went way down. Chow and Li wanted us to work hard and to enjoy the competition experience. Their attitude was always, "You're here to challenge yourself, but we want you to enjoy your work as well. This is too hard of a sport to stick with if you don't enjoy it."

My parents respected Chow and Li, and they supported them as well as me. Once, when I was at level 8, I was scheduled to compete in Kansas City. A bad blizzard had hit the area, and my parents were concerned—not just about me getting to the meet in bad weather, but about Chow having to make that long drive on his own.

Dad called my coach and told him, "I think we need to go together." A half hour later we met up with Chow, who followed us on I-35. The road conditions continued to get worse. Finally, we were detoured off the highway and onto a smaller road. It seemed everywhere we looked there were cars and semis in the ditches, and we could only inch along.

By the time we arrived for the competition, we were late. Fortunately, we weren't the only ones who'd been delayed by bad weather, so the start time was postponed for a half hour or so. I saw my parents and coaches pulling together like that time and time again, and because of that I was able to remain focused on training.

SHAWN JOHNSON

My mom and dad never missed a competition. Neither did Tori, my cousin—at least until I began competing internationally. She was the one who always did my hair for meets. Since about the only touch of individuality we're allowed in our appearance is our hair ribbon, she and I would spend extra time deciding which one I should wear during each competition. My Chow teammates never knew whether I'd show up in braids, cornrows, or a pigtail, but thanks to Tori, I always looked great. Eventually, the other parents began paying Tori to do their daughters' hair too.

When I was twelve, I had reached the highest junior level—10. I had to qualify at the state level, then at regionals, and then at nationals. This required hard work and a great deal of practice, but I made it to nationals.

The Women's Junior Olympic National Championships were held in Kissimmee, Florida, in April 2004. Though I placed in several events—second on floor; fourth in the all-around and on vault—the highlight was my win on the balance beam. I've always loved this event. For me, a daredevil, nothing gets the adrenaline pumping more than doing flips on a four-inch-wide beam. I ended up nailing my routine on the beam and winning the gold. In fact, one judge gave me a 9.9. At that time, I couldn't have scored higher than a 10.

I was thrilled, largely because I had wanted to do well for Li, who couldn't be there. After receiving my gold medal, I told Chow, "This medal is for her."

Because I came in fourth overall at the Florida meet, I received an invitation to attend the National Junior Camp at the US Olympic Training Center in Colorado Springs later that summer. Once there, I dared to wonder for the first time if I might someday have a chance to go after the biggest prize of all: Olympic gold.

27

Lesson I've Learned

So many people try to force success. In my sport, I've seen parents uproot and move their entire family, trying to find the perfect coach—someone who can take their son or daughter to the top. I'm grateful that my parents allowed things to progress on their own, rather than trying to make something happen. Find something you love, work hard at it, and keep your family a priority. Things just have a way of working out from there.

CHAPTER 4

INSPIRATION

Faith is taking the first step even when you don't see the whole staircase.
—*Martin Luther King Jr.*

"Get down from there," the guard yelled at my friend and me. We were climbing down a metal statue, but we froze as still as the sculpted figure when we saw the guard quickly approaching.

Though most of our time at the National Junior Camp had been spent practicing, Chow and I had joined another coach and gymnast and were taking advantage of some downtime to enjoy our impressive surroundings. The Olympic Training Center, the headquarters for the US Olympic Committee administration and the Olympic Training Center programs, was once an air force base. Now it's a state-of-the-art sports complex that makes you appreciate how much effort it takes to become an Olympic athlete.

That day, we were walking around the campus to see the Olympic flame and visit the gift shop. On our way, we saw the statue of a girl on a beam doing an arabesque.

"Look," I said, pointing up at her.

"Do you think we could get a photo?" my friend asked. "She's beautiful!"

Chow and the other coach were busy talking, so they stopped while we got out our cameras and climbed onto the statue and posed next to the girl. That's when we saw the guard running toward us across the parking lot. We clambered down the statue and were standing on the ground by the time he reached us. He tapped the sign, which read—very clearly—"Do Not Climb on Statue." This, of course, caused me and my training partner to break into a fit of giggles as we ran away, leaving the two coaches behind to politely apologize for our behavior.

This was my first time away from home without my parents, and I was a little homesick. The girls were great, and one of the older ones named Tiffany adopted me for the week and took care of everything I needed. I followed her around so much they called her "Tallz" and me "Smallz."

My coaches good-naturedly teased me since, at twelve, I was the youngest gymnast there. The dance teacher, Antonia, liked to single me out by calling me "baby" while instructing us in the dance steps. The other coaches called me Bamm-Bamm—after the Rubbles' tiny but tremendously strong offspring on *The Flintstones*.

We stayed in the Training Center's dorms, which I thought were amazing in spite of the fact that the bathroom and the showers were upstairs.

"Here," Tiffany said early in the week. She handed me a key to the room as I headed out. "You'll need this to get back into the room. You might want to just keep it for the week, or you'll be in big trouble if you need to go to the bathroom."

I took the key and clutched it tightly. I'd never had my own key before. Every time I'd gone out of town, my parents had traveled with me. They had always handled the details of getting in and out of our hotel room. This key was a big responsibility, and

I was intoxicated by the freedom. It was great being on campus. I particularly loved the cafeteria, where they fed over six hundred resident athletes and coaches who were hungry after practice and competition. The gigantic serving space had little booths where you could get all kinds of food—salads, pastas, grilled foods, deli items, and desserts. Really, it had anything you could imagine, so I loved going to the dining hall and trying a variety of foods.

Because the Olympic Games were going on in Athens while we were there, our training felt particularly significant. Every night in the dining hall, the athletes gathered around a big-screen TV while we ate our grilled chicken and salads. It was as if we were being allowed to see a glimpse of our future, if only we worked hard enough.

The star Olympian of those Games was a gymnast: Carly Patterson.

I watched in awe as she competed valiantly in the women's all-around, the most prestigious gymnastics event. In the Olympics, there's no higher honor than winning a gold in this competition, and only one American had done it before: Mary Lou Retton in 1984.

When Carly performed, she cast a spell. She captured the minds and hearts of Americans who were watching all over the nation. She also captured the imagination and heart of one particular athlete watching from that dining hall that night. I held my breath as she confidently performed on the bars and the beam.

As the national anthem played in her honor after she won the gold medal in the all-around, I thought, *One day, I want to be right there. On the podium, representing America and wearing a gold medal.*

Of course, that was improbable. I wasn't even "elite" yet. But I did have big dreams. That moment at the Training Center pushed me to work even harder once I was back in West Des Moines. I wanted to be the best in the world, but first I had to qualify as an elite athlete.

Only elite gymnasts get to compete on a national level. To become one, I had to go to an elite qualifier in Wisconsin. Chow began instructing me in the required floor routine, which had been created by a team of judges. Making all of us perform the same routine allowed the judges to more fairly evaluate the gymnasts' skill level and talent. Chow made me practice it until I had perfected every step.

When Chow and I got to Wisconsin, we were a little lost. But we had one thing going for us: I knew that routine forward and backward. When it was my turn to compete, I confidently strode out to the mat and began to perform. I hit every mark. When it was all over, I knew I'd nailed it. I threw my hands up into the air and caught Chow's eye. He beamed with pride.

Oddly, I didn't get a score immediately. In fact, one of the judges got up from her table and walked over to Chow. I had no idea what was going on, but she talked to him for a while. A little sheepishly, he came over to me and apologized.

"I'm sorry, Shawn," he began. "Apparently your routine wasn't right."

"What do you mean?" I asked, incredulous. "I nailed it!"

"Yes, you did," he said softly. "But it was the wrong routine. It was old."

"How old?"

"It was the one they used twelve years ago."

"Did they give you the wrong one?" I asked, a little concerned that I'd traveled to Wisconsin to be evaluated and suddenly wasn't even going to have a chance to qualify as an elite.

Chow put his hand on my shoulder. "I'm sorry, but I found that routine on the Internet. It was apparently the wrong one."

The judge was kind enough to teach me the routine on the floor right there in front of everyone. "If you can perform this now," she said, "you won't be penalized."

SHAWN JOHNSON

And so, with a very apologetic coach watching from the sidelines, I performed a brand-new routine. That wasn't the only difficulty I encountered at that qualifier. I just wasn't hitting any of my routines at the level I wanted and needed to. Going into my last event, I knew exactly what score I had to earn and figured I probably wouldn't qualify as an elite this time. When my final score was read, I was elated: with that number, I realized I'd qualified by .0025 points.

As soon as the judge said, "Congratulations, you made it," I turned and saw Tori. I ran right to her and gave her a big hug. I knew that she, as much as anyone, understood how much this achievement meant to me. I was now eligible to compete at the elite level—with the goal of earning a spot on the national team.

Lesson I've Learned

Looking up to someone who can inspire and motivate you is great, but you were made to be unique. Don't grow up wanting to be like somebody else. Instead, dare to be different and become your own person—the unique person God made you to be.

CHAPTER 5

THE SECRET VIDEO

Teachers open the door, but you must enter by yourself.
—*Chinese proverb*

IF GYMNASTICS HAD ROYALTY, Bela Karolyi would be king.

He is, of course, the mustachioed Romanian who first introduced the world to Nadia Comaneci, the gymnast who scored the first-ever perfect ten during the 1976 Olympics. Eight years later he coached Mary Lou Retton, the first American woman to win a gold medal in Olympic gymnastics (and more medals than any other athlete at the '84 Games).

Though quieter and lesser known to the general public, his wife, Martha, is an outstanding coach in her own right. The Karolyis married in Romania and began coaching there. In 1981, they brought the Romanian national team to the United States for a tour. Instead of flying back to Romania with the rest of

their team when the exposition ended, the Karolyis requested
and received political asylum.

A few years later, Bela bought forty acres in Texas as a hunt-
ing retreat. Soon he had added a gym and some camps, and the
Karolyis began holding camps for elite gymnasts. Though Bela
retired from active coaching after the 1996 Olympics, he and
Martha continued expanding their compound, which today
includes over two thousand acres. Every month, the best gymnasts in the country go there to receive training from these
famous coaches.

Now that I had achieved elite status, I was in a transition stage.
Getting to the point where I might have the opportunity to compete at the Olympic level was an elaborate, multistage progression. The next step was going to a camp so Bela and Martha could
evaluate me to make sure I was worthy of competing. It was a big,
intimidating process that I wasn't necessarily interested in or even
all that aware of. At that point, I was satisfied with having qualified
as an elite.

Coach Chow, however, wanted to make sure I reached my full
potential. After analyzing my competition, he decided I should be
introduced to Martha Karolyi—even though neither of us had ever
met her. One day, Chow started bringing in a camera and filming
me doing different skills in each event. I figured he was doing this
for recruitment videos or college videos. I never guessed he was up
to something that would change the course of my life forever.

Chow did not edit the tapes he'd recorded of me; he wanted
Martha to see exactly what I was capable of. A few weeks later
he sent her the tape, along with a letter that said, "Martha, you
should take a look at the kid on this film. I think she will be
helping Team USA."

I knew nothing about the tape, and my parents knew nothing
about it. A few weeks later, I went to the gym and lined up on the

mat like we did every day before practice began. But on that particular occasion, Chow had a big package in his hand.

"This is for you, Shawn," he said, walking over to me and extending it in my direction. I took the box hesitantly. Why would he single
me out with a gift? It wasn't my birthday.

"I just wanted to take this chance to tell everyone this at the same
time so we can all congratulate Shawn. She's been accepted to the
Karolyis' camp."

What? I was in shock because I had no idea that this was even
a possibility (or that I'd even applied).

Martha Karolyi had invited me to a developmental camp. These
camps mix national team members along with those gymnasts who
show promise of making it to that level. After a full week of conditioning and training, I'd be able to take part in a mock meet, where
Martha and other coaches would give me feedback. Of course, it
was an amazing opportunity, but I would have been nervous had I
known Coach Chow had written to her.

By now I was in middle school at Indian Hills, and my life
was mostly like that of my friends. Sometimes after school my dad
would pick me up from Chow's and drive me straight to a school
football game. He and my mom didn't want me to miss school-
related activities.

At home, Dad would take me out to the cul-de-sac, where he
taught me how to ride a motorbike—a little Honda CT70, to be
exact. He'd laugh as I sputtered along, but I actually got to be pretty
good at it and learned to drive one with a clutch.

I was always under the watchful eye of my parents and enjoyed
my quiet, peaceful life with them in Iowa, though my journal
reflected a normal girl's concerns:

> My parents are both very protective of me and never want
> to see anything happen to me. I guess I don't appreciate

that as much as I should. I sometimes get mad at them for not letting me go to the mall alone or with a friend and for not letting me have a cell phone until I prove that I'm responsible enough. But I think about all they are doing, and it really makes sense. Everything they do is for a goal and has a reason. I don't like making my bed, but I have to do it every day. It's just a part of life. I try not to develop a competing plan against my parents, because their plan is just perfect for me right now.

My parents wanted my life to be in balance. As I went through childhood, Mom encouraged me to "fill up my plate" with the right amount of activities, hobbies, schoolwork, friends, and other relationships. But she made sure all of these were in the right proportion. Unlike the elite gymnasts whose forty-hour-a-week training schedules necessitate homeschooling or private tutors, at this point I was training twenty to twenty-five hours a week. Fortunately, Chow had the same idea about what mattered most in my life: "Education is number one," he'd tell me. "Gymnastics is number two."

Now Martha Karolyi was giving me the chance to take my gymnastics to the next level . . . the very highest. I'd dreamed of wearing a leotard with the letters *USA* emblazoned on the front. Like most Americans, I was patriotic and loved the Fourth of July. We'd always spend that holiday on our boat with our friends. We would all tie our boats up and grill steaks and crab legs. In the evening, we'd set off fireworks over the water before the big ones were set off in the nearby city. I loved celebrating the day because I loved celebrating my country. The thought of representing the USA in competition was almost beyond my imagination.

"Are you sure you're ready for this?" my mom and dad asked

me in various ways at various times. Suddenly, their desire for me to have a balanced life, not given to extremes, was threatened. In fact, my parents are the most normal people you'll ever meet and have always told me the decision to keep competing in gymnastics was completely mine. I knew they wanted me to be happy, not necessarily a happy gymnast. Now that I'd progressed to this status, I was doing more and more difficult moves . . . a development my mom in particular didn't really enjoy. I later learned that Mom prayed a lot for me during competitions. But she wasn't asking God to help me win—she was just asking him to keep me from getting hurt!

"You have to decide whether to go to the Karolyis' camp based on what *you* want to do," she told me. There are so many stereotypes about "stage moms"—mothers who push their children into certain sports or hobbies in order to vicariously live through them. My mom couldn't have been further from that. She would have preferred that we stay home together and read books or watch TV, not go all over the world for competitions. But more than anything, she wanted me to live my dreams. So she allowed me to make the decision.

"I want to do it," I said. "I want to be the best, and the Karolyis train the best." Martha's input was critical for up-and-coming gymnasts. As national team coordinator for USA Gymnastics, she selected athletes for competitions, determined lineups at the top meets, and made recommendations about skills and the composition of routines.

Once they knew I was committed to advancing, my parents supported me totally, with one condition: that I follow my coaches' rules out of respect for them. They'd never let me be disrespectful of Chow and Li; the same would be true of the Karolyis.

Lesson I've Learned

Life will be richer once you find your passion—but never lose sight of everything else. If one activity becomes everything to you, you may have nothing left if you lose it. To keep my life in balance, my parents didn't want my schedule to be lopsided, too heavily weighted with one activity. They encouraged me to fill my time with the right amount of hobbies, schoolwork, and relationships—in the right proportion.

CHAPTER 6

NOT YOUR
AVERAGE SUMMER CAMP

Whatever your 100 percent looks like, give it.
—*Lance Armstrong*

IF THE ROAD TO ELITE competition had been long and winding, the drive from Houston to Karolyi's Camp accurately symbolized that journey. After flying into Houston, Coach Chow and I met up with four other gymnasts. By the time we claimed our luggage and got into our rental van, I was completely wound up.

"How long does it take to get there?" I asked.

"About an hour," our driver said.

That didn't keep me from asking over and over during the drive, "Are we almost there yet?"

I wasn't sure what to expect. I'd been to the Olympic Training Center, a sprawling, high-tech facility. Perhaps the camp was similar.

No matter what it looked like, it had to be wonderful. The Karolyi ranch is where Olympic athletes are made. After the 2000 Sydney Olympics, where the American women won no medals, the Karolyis created a semi-centralized training system to help increase esprit de corps among our nation's gymnasts. In the past, the

American team would sometimes meet each other for the first time at the airport on the way to the competition, which is a tough way to build a sense of camaraderie. Members of the national team still live and train at home with their own coaches. However, every four weeks, they meet at the Karolyi ranch with the other girls on the team for training camps run by Martha. This allows gymnasts to know how they stack up against the other athletes—and Martha's standards—while also fostering team unity.

Would I be one of those girls who made the monthly trek to who-knows-where? The center, sixty miles north of Houston, is definitely off the beaten path. We drove on a two-lane road out to New Waverly, Texas—which has a population of less than one thousand. We made a pit stop at the local grocery store, which was evidently a tradition for every vanload of gymnasts and coaches coming from the airport.

My anticipation was growing more with every passing mile. And it seemed like there were many, many miles. We passed cow pastures and barns, until the paved road eventually turned to gravel. And the camp was *still* nowhere in sight.

"Are we there yet?" I continued asking about every ten minutes. I looked through the windows of the van. I couldn't see any stores or houses. In fact, I noticed, there weren't even light poles or telephone poles. Nothing. I just saw mile after mile of trees and cow pastures. Eventually, the two-lane gravel road became an old logging road, a narrow path in a forest. I sat in the back and prayed for dear life that another car wouldn't come flying around the next bend and hit us head-on.

Eventually, the one-lane road ended at the Karolyi ranch. We were welcomed by a yellow sign that read, "Welcome to Karolyi's Waverly Hills Camp: Home of Olympic and World Champions." When I read those words, I knew my career wouldn't end in that steel building. It was just about to start.

I was a little surprised at what I saw. The camp wasn't high tech. I didn't see much but several buildings, which I soon learned were the gym, the cafeteria, and one long cabin with twelve little dorm rooms that Bela had built. A little farther back were the cabins of the workers and the house where the Karolyis lived.

The first day of training, I walked into the gym and was surprised at how no-frills it was. Huge garage doors were opened on days with good weather to provide light and circulation. This wood-paneled place had gotten a lot of use. This was where Mary Lou Retton and Kerri Strug had trained, and the whole gym was filled with posters and autographed photos of athletes who had trained there. There was a poster of Dominique Dawes, a member of the gold medal–winning "Magnificent Seven" at the '96 Olympic Games. There were photos of Bela and Mary Lou, posing at the center, with her thousand-watt smile in full force. There was a framed photograph of Bela carrying the injured Kerri to the podium at the 1996 Olympics. It was signed, "Bela, I really appreciate all you've done for me. I'll always be grateful. Love, Kerri." There were also numerous trophies, posters, and other memorabilia to commemorate the world and Olympic competitors from the United States who have been shaped by Bela and Martha.

At the camp, there was literally nothing to do but gymnastics. We ate and slept gymnastics, since we weren't allowed to leave the camp and nobody was allowed to come in. (Not that they could have found it!) Spending a week concentrating solely on gymnastics was very helpful and instructive, but it was *not* easy.

Six days of the week (and sometimes seven) we got up early and did a complete training workout. I remember all of us doing the same movements in unison under Martha's watchful eye—squatting every few steps, jumping into a half turn, leaping into a full turn, shuffling our feet, pointing our toes. The exercises looked simple at first but progressed into more and more complicated movements.

We ran around the square mat; we kicked our legs out to one side and then the other; we did crunches and sits-ups. After we moved from the mats, we did jumps on the vault, repeatedly. We hung from the high bars and did sit-ups. We did pull-ups with our arms in different positions to work out different muscles. Then we'd break up and work on our routines—floor, bars, and beam—with our coaches from home.

Martha and her national team staff walked among the groups, letting us know if our toes weren't pointed in precisely the right way or if our arms were not extended perfectly. At the end of each session, we would all line up according to height, arms behind our backs, and say in unison: "Thank you, Martha, coaches, and national staff! Good-bye."

After our morning session, we broke for lunch to eat meals like salad and chicken in the cafeteria. It wasn't very glamorous, and we were convinced they injected everything with fiber.

Practice resumed in the afternoons, when we'd try to perfect our routines and learn new moves. During these practices we really tried to push ourselves further than we'd ever gone. We'd break for dinner around seven. After that, our team doctor would send a trainer so we could receive a massage at the end of the night. By nine, we were done for the day.

As intense as the training was, I loved being able to relax with my gymnastics friends after practice. We'd do one another's nails, makeup, and hair. We'd get on the Internet and listen to music or watch movies in our rooms. Of course, by nighttime we were exhausted and were aware that the next day's practice would begin early, so we never got too crazy.

Bela didn't come to the gym very often. Instead, he spent most of his time managing the ranch facilities. I'll never forget the first time I saw him.

It was during one of our weekly formal competitions. Even if we weren't in competition shape, we'd prepare our routines and compete against each other. Not only did it allow us to compare ourselves to each other, it also helped us get into the competition mind-set.

I was preparing to go up on the beam when I saw the door open, and Bela strolled in. He was bigger than I expected, and I tried not to be distracted by him. Apparently Martha had told Bela about me, because he sat down to watch our competition. As the other gymnasts noticed his presence, everyone got even more serious about their routines. The energy in the room skyrocketed, though the gymnasts pretended not to realize he was watching.

I jumped up on the beam and did my routine. I can't remember how I did, though I'm sure if you'd asked me at the time I would have told you I nailed it. When I finished, I heard Bela cheering for me in his thick Romanian accent.

Wow, I thought. *Bela Karolyi just yelled for me.* I was on top of the world and felt invincible.

Apparently Bela has always loved animals, so his camp is like one big zoo. Huge peacocks roamed around in the field right outside our dorms, mingling with groups of turkeys. There were also mules, camels, donkeys, chickens, and geese. Oh, and to make things more interesting, there were snakes everywhere. Bela told us to make sure we closed the toilet at night because snakes sometimes crawl up the plumbing.

You'd think that would be enough to keep you from going to the bathroom at night. But once I woke up in the middle of the night and really *had to go*. In my dorm, there were three beds and a little bathroom with a toilet and another bathroom with showers. The other girls were asleep, so I tiptoed through the dark and walked into the bathroom. Once the door was closed and I could turn on the light without waking my friends, I flipped on the switch.

I almost wished I hadn't.

Because that's when I saw the biggest cockroaches I'd ever seen, crawling on the wall right next to me. When they say everything is bigger in Texas, they're serious. I started screaming my head off. I was rooming with Nastia Liukin at the time, so I ran out of the bathroom and jumped on top of her bed.

"Are you okay?" she said, sitting straight up after being awakened so abruptly.

"There are enormous cockroaches in there!" I screamed.

Unfortunately, we were both terrified of bugs. Absolutely terrified. So we made our other roommate get up and kill them. There was no way we could go to bed thinking about those cockroaches crawling all over us.

To prepare for my first elite competition, I began making monthly trips to the Karolyi ranch. While I was there, I worked even harder than I did at home because I got to see gymnasts from all over the country who were just as good as I was—or even better. Martha assessed our performance and gave us a list of things to focus on over the next month. Every time I left the camp, I had a new resolve to become a top gymnast.

I knew how well I measured up at the ranch. But how would I compare to the rest of the world?

Lesson I've Learned

When it comes to your passion, set your sights high—higher than you think possible right now so you have something to work for. At the same time, you must believe you *can* achieve what you set out to do.

CHAPTER 7

"WHO IS *THAT* GIRL?"

Go confidently in the direction of your dreams!
Live the life you've imagined.
—*Henry David Thoreau*

It didn't take me long to find out how I ranked among other
top gymnasts. Just a few months after returning home from Texas,
I packed my bags and headed to Virginia Beach for the 2005 US
Classic, which serves as the final qualifying event for the Visa National
Championships. This was my first competition as an elite, and I
couldn't wait to make my debut. Perhaps it was good that Martha
had already scrutinized every one of my movements in Texas, because
when we arrived at the arena, cameras were everywhere.

I felt a bit like a rock star! When I did my routine, a camera followed me and filmed my every move. Far from being intimidated,
I was energized by the cameras. While I was naturally shy, I loved
performing gymnastics. It was the one thing I was completely confident doing. I thought, *Watch me, world!*

Of course, "the world" didn't know who this "me" was. I was the
new kid on the block, and nobody had ever seen me. I remember the

other gymnasts and coaches looking at me with quizzical expressions. *Who is* that *girl?* they seemed to be thinking.

Their reaction to me was understandable. To them, I had come out of nowhere. The gymnastics world is one large, extended family, and everyone usually knows everyone else . . . including where they came from, who their coach is, and what their talent level is. There is a typical progression to get to this level. Most aspiring gymnasts start out in TOPs, a talent search and educational program for promising young female gymnasts and their coaches. They begin going to a summer camp at the Karolyi ranch when they're seven; then they compete at certain qualifiers. I hadn't gone through those steps, so I'd never had the chance to interact with most of the elite gymnasts and their coaches until the Virginia Beach meet.

I think they were a little surprised when I placed third in the all-around.

It's almost unheard of for an unknown to perform well and even place in an elite meet. It was so amazing to leave with a medal. I loved competing!

Just a few weeks later, I was on my way to Indianapolis for my first Visa Championships. During the all-around competition, I fell from the beam. At that moment, I had to put much of Chow's teaching into play: a mistake isn't fatal unless you choose to dwell on it and let it distract you during the next event. In the end, I finished tenth, earning the final spot on USA Gymnastics' junior national team.

Being picked last for a team is sometimes terrible, like being the last person standing against the wall when the fourth grade class is selecting dodgeball teams. However, in 2005, I'd already qualified as an elite, gone to Karolyi's Camp, and been selected to compete at the nationals. And now I'd made it onto the national team!

My parents and I attended our first national team meeting the very next morning, where we received general instructions about expectations and scheduling. At the end of the breakfast meeting, the officials handed out international assignments for meets held all over the globe. After handing out the big competitions to the seniors, they said, "Okay, we have two assignments for juniors."

I couldn't believe my ears. I'd barely made the team, and now I might have the chance to travel for my country? They handed the first assignment to the top juniors, and then they said they had a second meet in Belgium. "This one is for you," they said as they handed the assignment to my teammate Ivana Hong. And then . . . "This one is for you, Shawn."

My parents looked stunned. I didn't even have a passport! I could see the concern in my mom's eyes. Though she didn't say a word, I could hear her voice in my head saying, *My baby's going to Belgium?* Yet USA Gymnastics knows that low-profile international meets like this one are good places to throw newbies like me. I could either bomb without major repercussions or I could do great while gaining valuable experience and confidence.

I could barely contain my joy. As I waited for the day to come when I'd go to the airport and head overseas, I wrote in my journal every single day about the same topic: my uniform. "I have a week and two days before I go to Belgium. I'm so excited but am also really scared, too. I wonder where I'll be staying, and I wonder what my leotard will look like. It should come in the mail within two days."

The next day I wrote more of the same: "I can't believe I've made it this far. Sometimes, I wish I was still just rec, when there was less pressure, but I love everything that has come with this success. I've been having dreams about what my leotard is going to look like, but my stuff still hasn't arrived. In my dream, the leotard didn't look very good, so I was disappointed. I hope that doesn't really happen in real life."

Now that I was traveling with the national team, we thought it was the right time to set up a website for me. I felt like I'd finally arrived when I saw it online for the first time. One little girl had already sent me an e-mail.

"Dear Shawn," she wrote. "I am having trouble with my back handspring. Can you give me some pointers?"

Does this technically qualify as fan mail? I wondered. I counted it as one, but I didn't know how to advise her by e-mail when a back handspring really needs to be tweaked in person. I didn't write back, and I felt horrible about that. I wrote in my journal, "I hope she isn't mad."

Finally, two days before I was scheduled to leave, the box with my uniform arrived. I nearly tore it out of my mom's hands.

"Let me see!" I cried as I ripped it open, leaving packing remnants on the living room floor. The box contained three pairs of pants, three pairs of shorts, two pairs of shoes (tennis shoes and sandals), two pairs of underwear, three pairs of socks, four T-shirts, a silky shirt, a long-sleeved shirt, a winter vest, a gym bag, and seven leotards (four for warm-up and three for competition). I was elated.

I was thirteen years old and had been given the honor of wearing a leotard emblazoned with "USA." When I put it on in my bedroom and looked in the mirror, I felt a tremendous sense of pride in my country.

The day before we left for the Top Gym meet in Belgium, I had my first interview with a gymnastics magazine. I couldn't believe that the editors wanted to talk to me, but I enjoyed every second of the exchange. My interviewer asked me a few questions about what it was like to be on the national team. Though I can't quite remember what I told her, I probably said that traveling internationally for the junior national team was one of the biggest honors of my life.

I felt a little strange getting on the airplane with my coaches and teammates but without Mom and Dad. That didn't mean they wouldn't see me compete, however. Normally, parents don't attend the international meets; in fact, because many coaches see them as a distraction, they're often discouraged from attending. However, my parents were not going to allow me to travel to a different country while they stayed home. They got their own airline tickets, booked their own hotel across town, and bought tickets for the meet. So while I nestled into my seat on the airplane, I was comforted to know they'd be in the stands for my first international competition. I hoped I'd be able to spot them.

I was thrilled to be in Belgium, although I got homesick when I couldn't reach my parents by phone. I hoped they weren't worried about me. Our accommodations weren't five-star, to say the least, and I couldn't even get the shower to work. There was one perk, however. The dining hall had the best bread rolls I've ever had in my entire life. We always had to be very careful about what we ate in front of our coaches, but when Ivana and I went down to dinner, we made sure to stock up on the rolls. Throughout our meal, we'd stuff them into our gym bags and pockets. When we got back to the room, we'd eat about a dozen apiece!

I actually ended up taking first place in the all-around, vault, and floor in Belgium, but my main memories of that trip are of the USA leotard . . . and those dinner rolls. This competition represented a turning point of another sort as well. As my routines became more challenging, I began to pray for protection before every meet: "God, please watch over me. Keep me healthy and safe." Like my mom, I understood that, at this level, gymnastics is a dangerous sport.

When I returned home from Belgium, I felt a little different, a little more grown-up than I'd been when I had left. While my friends were thinking about the latest reality TV show or home-work assignment, I was thinking about new moves I wanted to nail and competitions I wanted to qualify for. None of my friends at school really understood the gymnastics side of me. They just knew that I was exceptionally strong, always went to the gym after school, and had less free time on the weekends than they did. But I largely tried to keep my two lives separate, a surprisingly easy task since no one was all that interested in what I was doing when I wasn't sitting at my desk or hanging out with friends.

I'd gone from the winner's podium at the competition to the school cafeteria lunch line, where I hoped there would still be some white milk by the time I got to the end. At competitions I loved the feeling of testing the limits of my strength, agility, and flexibility. It may sound silly, but once I was back home, I felt a little like Clark Kent, just trying to fit in at school and making sure I slid into my seat before the bell rang.

My parents were good at helping me look ahead and find a way to fit in the normal teenage milestones. Because they encouraged me to take driver's ed as soon as I was eligible to do so, I was able to finish the course before my competition schedule became too full to fit it in. Months before that my dad had begun teaching me to drive. When he got home from work, he'd park his truck in the street and call me outside so I could drive the truck into the driveway.

When I was fourteen, I got an unexpected invitation. Bernie Saggau, the longtime head of the Iowa High School Athletic Association, invited my parents and me to meet him at the Iowa Hall of Pride, an interactive educational facility that celebrates notable Iowans in athletics, music, broadcasting, and other endeavors.

Bernie had heard of me from his two granddaughters, who were also training at Chow's Gym. He thought I had the potential to be a standout in gymnastics and a role model for girls. The Iowa Hall of Pride attracts thousands of schoolchildren to downtown Des Moines every year, but on the night we met with Bernie and the hall's director, Jack Lashier, we were the only visitors.

Bernie and Jack walked us to the area where they told us they wanted to create an exhibit highlighting my achievements. Mine would be right next to the display on PGA Masters' winner Zach Johnson—thus, they could call us the "Johnson and Johnson" exhibit.

I was nearly speechless. "You're going to do that for me?" I asked. "I haven't won anything yet."

Bernie smiled. "I don't care. You are a tremendous role model for young girls, and I think you have the potential to be Iowa's greatest gymnast."

I've always been proud to say I'm from Iowa. I don't think there's a more close-knit community anywhere, so it was an honor to be included in my home state's Hall of Pride. My parents, coaches, family friends, teachers, and I were interviewed on camera so a video montage of my life and gymnastics career could be created. Sculptor Rick Stewart of Newton, Iowa, was commissioned to create a sculpture of me on a balance beam. While the exhibit didn't open for a couple of years, I think Bernie and Jack were glad they began working on it when they did. Over the coming months, I had less and less time to concentrate on anything other than school and gymnastics.

By early 2006, I was focused on preparing for the Visa Championships as a member of the junior national team. That year the championships would be held in St. Paul in August, and I saw my opportunity to make a statement. As I've mentioned, gymnasts don't have many ways to distinguish their appearances. When competing as a national team member, my teammates and I wore identical leotards. However, a few times each year I had to compete as an individual to requalify for the national team. For those competitions, Coach Chow encouraged my desire to design my own leotard.

I'd start with an outline of a bare leotard and then provide specific instructions, not only about color and fabrics, but about what stitching, "jewels," and neckline should be used. GK Elite Sportswear provides a custom design service, so they'd create the leotard according to my exact specifications. My favorite was the one I designed for the competition in St. Paul. My name was written in Chinese characters on my sleeve. It was my way of expressing my goal to make the Olympic team that would be headed to Beijing. When people saw it, they assumed I'd done it to honor Chow. Of course, this was also true. I was so proud to be making the journey with such a great coach, someone who was willing to go out of his way to help me achieve my full potential.

Yes, I had ambitious goals, but I delivered by coming in first in the all-around at the Visa Championships. I was still a junior, which simply meant I was under fifteen years old. (To compete at the senior level, gymnasts generally must be sixteen. The exception is the year just prior to the next summer Olympics, when fifteen-year-olds are also eligible to compete as seniors.) The neat thing about my scores that year—and the thing that surprised everyone in attendance— was that they were higher than those of the winning senior-level gymnasts. I was thrilled, and people began describing me as the top up-and-coming junior, the gymnast to watch.

This championship was special for another reason: it was the first time I met Mary Lou Retton, who presented the medals. I'd always looked up to her because of her style, her character, and the fact that, like me, she's never been afraid to be her own person and stand out. I was thrilled to shake her hand after she presented me with my medal, but I was even more pleased when she came over to me later and showed genuine interest in my story.

The media has often compared me to Mary Lou, and frankly, that's a big compliment. I love that she has remained down to earth, true to her own goals, and committed to her family. I hope the same will always be true of me as well.

Lesson I've Learned

"Love never gives up, never loses faith, is always hopeful, and endures through every circumstance" (1 Corinthians 13:7).

CHAPTER 8

WATCH ME, WORLD!

I am building a fire, and every day I train, I add more fuel.
At just the right moment, I light the match.
—*Mia Hamm*

EVEN AFTER THESE EARLY SUCCESSES, my life hadn't changed very much. Coach Chow is a firm believer in a training program that allows for life outside the gym—something he never had growing up. That meant that I continued to practice about twenty-five hours a week, including four hours after school each day and another five or six hours on Saturdays. The intensity increased as my coaches helped me set and work on new goals. They even helped me come up with key words that would keep me focused on exactly how I wanted to perform each skill—simple phrases like "stay under control." Chow told me he was constantly amazed by my ability to listen to his correction and then incorporate about 90 percent of it the next time I performed that skill. That ability, he said, was rare and would help set me apart from other gymnasts.

Chow and Li had always taught me to recognize the difference between practicing and performing. It's relatively easy to learn and execute new skills in the gym. I wanted to learn all the time, so that came easy to me. But they reminded me that competition demands much more. You have to be able to overcome your nerves and ignore the spectators and cameras while performing at your highest level.

I took those lessons to heart, and they became important as 2007 began. In March I was in Jacksonville, Florida, for the Tyson American Cup. As I warmed up in the arena before the competition, I was able to tune out the activity around me.

Boom, boom, boom. I was hitting my flips hard on the balance beam and didn't notice a woman and a USA Gymnastics official pause for a moment to watch me. The woman with the official was Sheryl Shade, a former marketing executive with Walt Disney Pictures and Hawaiian Tropic who, about ten years before, had founded her own firm. Shade Global specializes in representing Olympic athletes and documentary filmmakers, among others. Sheryl had already heard some buzz about me. After seeing me in person and watching as I took the all-around title, she decided she'd better get in touch with my coaches quickly.

Immediately after the American Cup, Sheryl e-mailed Coach Chow to express her interest in talking with me and my parents. Chow told her he thought that would be wise; however, my parents resisted at first. In fact, my mom refused to even talk with her. After all, why would *I* need an agent? Besides that, my mom wasn't sure what to think of New York agents.

My dad agreed to talk with Sheryl, but he, too, was skeptical. For six weeks, he and Sheryl talked about once a week, and each time my dad asked her more questions. Finally, he called to suggest that Sheryl fly in to Des Moines to meet our family. After meeting at Chow's, we had a great conversation over salads at a casual restaurant; in fact, I connected with her from the start.

It took a bit longer for Sheryl to convince my parents that she could play a vital role in my career. In particular, given my young age, she could help us determine whether I should go professional or retain my amateur status and remain eligible to compete in NCAA college gymnastics. My parents ultimately decided it was in my best interest to have a pro like Sheryl help me navigate these options. Though Sheryl handles many of my "business" decisions, my parents and I now think of her as family, and we trust her completely.

In July 2007, I headed to the Pan American Games in Rio de Janeiro, Brazil. I'd never been part of an event like it. There were more than five thousand athletes from all over the Americas, and participants competed in over three hundred events. The spectators were loud and enthusiastic—more like a soccer crowd than a typical gymnastics audience. People painted their faces and blew air horns to distract us. They threw Mardi Gras beads and bottles in the stands.

Some athletes might have been intimidated by this scene, but I wasn't. In fact, I was invigorated. There I was with my teammates, ready to compete in front of people who were yelling, stomping their feet, blowing whistles, and generally trying to mess with my mind. But they weren't able to rattle me. I felt like I could do anything, and once again, I was crowned all-around champion. Plus, I helped lead my country to the team title. I felt like I was on top of the world, but I knew I hadn't gotten there by myself.

As our national anthem played, I invited my teammates Rebecca Bross and Ivana Hong to join me on the podium's top spot. I knew they had worked just as hard as I had and deserved that spotlight as much as anyone. As I stood there listening to "The Star-Spangled Banner," I realized that these games would be one of the highlights of my career.

About a month later, I was in San Jose for the 2007 Visa Championships, which would determine the national champion in

women's artistic and rhythmic gymnastics. Because the Olympics
were coming up a year later, I had been classified as a senior competitor in February, shortly after I turned fifteen. This competition
was the first qualifier for the World Championships, but I wasn't
more nervous than usual. I looked at these meets as the place to
show everyone what I'd been working on, to push my body to
its limits. The pressure didn't faze me. Instead, it clarified my
thoughts and allowed me to concentrate fully on the task at hand.
I won the gold in the all-around.

As I stood on that podium, I couldn't believe how far I'd come.
But I was about to go a lot further.

Placing first at nationals allowed me to go to the World
Championships in Germany later that fall. In our sport, winning
this competition carries more prestige than medaling at the
Olympics. To compete at the Olympics, a gymnast must be representing a country. This means that sometimes very good gymnasts
from small countries are left out because those nations don't have
enough gymnasts to qualify as a team. Conceivably, a girl could be
the best all-around in the world but be unable to compete at the
Olympic level. Though it's not as publicized as the Olympics and
doesn't have the same hallowed history, the world competition truly
determines the best gymnasts in the world.

In addition to competing individually, I would be part of the
USA's national team. We weren't favored to win the team all-
around. China was expected to dominate, but we had other plans.

The American team had come for a battle. We fought Romania
and China for the gold medal, all the way down to the very last
event. I was the anchor on beam, which is supposed to be the most
important position. Amazingly, I fell. In a team competition, you
really can't make a single mistake. I was so upset because I felt that I'd
disappointed all of my team members and, in fact, the whole country.
However, our team captain, Alicia Sacramone, reminded us that if we

won the floor, the gold would still be ours. We really came through on the floor: I hit every single landing, and so did everybody else. In the end, we pulled ahead of China to win the team gold medal.

We'd been working together for so long that when we finally got ahold of that gold medal, nothing in the world could have felt better. We hugged and cried and shared the moment as a true team.

A couple of days later, I competed in the individual all-around. The winner of this event would go home with the most coveted medal and title in gymnastics . . . world champion. Only three American women had managed to win that title before: Chellsie Memmel, Shannon Miller, and Kim Zmeskal.

I hit every routine and ended up winning. I had gone from an up-and-coming junior to the best gymnast in the world in one year. It was unbelievable.

Not every moment of the world competition was picture-perfect, however. This was my first experience with a grueling, Olympic-length meet, so competing day after day after day was a little challenging. During the event finals, which happened a few days later, I competed on the beam and floor. That day, when I went up for beam, I fell twice in the same routine. This, of course, is unheard of. If you fall, you fall. But normally you don't fall twice . . . especially in the event finals. This was *my* event. I'm not sure I'd ever been so devastated.

I had an hour to be in the practice gym to warm up before competing on the floor finals. I'll never forget going back into the training gym and seeing Chow standing there.

He looked like he was in shock, but he collected himself before he spoke.

"Mistakes are mistakes," he said to me kindly. He wasn't mad at all, just disappointed. "Something was simply off."

I started bawling. He let me have my space for a little bit, then he came back to me to encourage me to regain my competition mind-set. "You know, things happen. Mistakes happen. But it's time to pick yourself up. You have another event."

I went out there with my head held high. I'd made it this far with great parents and a supportive coach. And so, when it was time for me to do my floor routine, I had no fear, doubt, or embarrassment over the mistakes I'd made.

I ended up with the gold in that event, as well as the Longines Prize for Elegance, which celebrates the athlete who has demonstrated the "most remarkable elegance" in the course of the world competitions. It was a great honor, especially since I've never really thought of myself that way. I'm regularly described as energetic and powerful, and I've even been called a spark plug, but this was the first time I'd been described as elegant.

When I returned home, my parents and I were startled by the increasing interest in me. I was introduced to the nation almost by accident. Sheryl had just returned from the World Championships when she met with an ABC News executive producer, Tom Yellin, about a documentary project. When he found out she'd just returned from Stuttgart, he mentioned hearing about the "small girl" who'd surprised everyone by winning the all-around. Sheryl told him my name and said she represented me.

Yellin thought for a moment and then explained that the news team would soon be meeting to choose the ABC Person of the Week. While it looked as if they would select either a politician or another world leader that week, he thought they should consider me as well. A day or so later, he called Sheryl to tell her the group had chosen me over the other two being considered.

There was only one problem: they needed to film on Thursday so the piece would be ready for Friday's newscast. I told Sheryl that I had already agreed to be ball girl for the football team after school on Thursday. ABC worked around that; they ended up taking footage of me on the sidelines of the football field, as well as in the gym.

Charlie Gibson introduced the Person of the Week segment this way: "She's a high school sophomore from an Iowa suburb—at first glance a typical good Midwest kid who likes text messaging, giggling with friends, who has a bunch of cats and dogs. And—oh yes—she's a world champion."

After a film clip showed me at work in the gym, Gibson mentioned that my devotion to my sport had brought "balance in life," noting that my hours of training helped me be disciplined and make good choices about how to spend the remaining hours of each day. The piece closed with my advice to others aspiring to rise to the top of their sport or discipline: "You can't really work hard if you don't have fun and make sure you're doing what your heart wants you to."[1]

Not long after the ABC Person of the Week segment aired, my congressman, Rep. Leonard Boswell, introduced and helped pass a resolution in the US House of Representatives to congratulate me on my world championship. And to top it off, Governor Chet Culver officially welcomed me home from Germany at the Iowa State Historical Building and named October 17, 2007, "Shawn Johnson Day." I stood a little taller when he called me a "role model for thousands of girls in Iowa and millions more around the country and the world, [who] represents herself, her family, her state, and her nation with grace and dignity."[2] I was then presented with a framed Congressional Record from Congressman Boswell and a letter from cyclist Lance Armstrong, one of my favorite athletes.

That same day, Adidas, an official sponsor of the USA Gymnastics team and the 2008 Beijing Olympics team, announced its major sponsorship deal with me. Agreements with Coca-Cola, McDonald's, and Hy-Vee soon followed.

As I stood there wearing my red, white, and blue warm-up suit with Chow and Li, it just felt surreal, like the governor was describing someone else. I looked out into the crowd and saw so many friends and family. I smiled, grateful that they had come out to celebrate with me that day. Something about finally being home, seeing old friends, and being among fellow Iowans made me really appreciate my home state.

What a season I'd had! In 2007, I placed first in every single competition I participated in. But there was one goal, one medal that I was still eyeing—though I'd have to make it to Beijing first.

Lesson I've Learned

As long as you've done your best, making mistakes doesn't matter. You and I are human; we will mess up. What counts is learning from your mistakes and getting back up when life has knocked you down.

CHAPTER 9

A CAST AND SOME POWER TOOLS

Pain is temporary. Quitting lasts forever.

—*Lance Armstrong*

By the time I returned home from Germany, the buzz had begun. People began speculating that I would definitely make the Olympic team, though I kept myself from believing it was a sure thing. My parents had taught me not to take success for granted, and I never assumed I'd be able to compete at the Olympic level. It seemed like a bubble, one that might break if I reached for it too quickly.

On top of that, I finally had to face one nagging concern after a year of unbelievable success—I had begun feeling severe pain in one leg. Like all competitive gymnasts, I had had to deal with the occasional twisted ankle or sore wrist. However, I knew that this leg pain, which I began feeling before Worlds, was different. Until I got home from Germany, however, I didn't have the time (or the heart) to investigate why it hurt. I took some Advil, put heat on it, and didn't let on that there was anything wrong. Based on the results I achieved at Worlds, I knew I'd made the right choice.

When I returned home to Des Moines, I went straight to the doctor. The pain had gotten so intense, I knew I had to have it checked out. After examining my leg, my doctor gave me the bad news.

"You have a stress fracture to your shin," he explained. I let out a tremendous sigh, which is when I realized I'd been holding my breath.

"It's actually very typical," he said. "You've had a hard, long year, pounding every little ounce out of your body." Apparently stress fractures happen when muscles become fatigued or overloaded. Since gymnasts frequently overuse their muscles, they get tired and can't absorb the shock of the repeated impact that they endure sometimes hundreds of times per day, six or seven days a week.

"We're going to have to cast it," he said. I bit my lip as I listened to him. Every day of missed practice would put me behind in my preparations for the Olympics. "And you need to stay off of it for about twelve weeks."

I knew I was fortunate. I'd sort of prided myself on not being injury-prone. On top of that, Chow and Li had devised a training program that had kept me remarkably free from injury for nearly ten years. While the doctor's recommendations made good sense, I definitely was not going to take several weeks off.

Gymnasts simply do not miss practice. I've seen girls come to practice with ligament injuries, fractures, and the flu. If something terrible happened that took you out of the gym for a week or two, you'd be done. At least that's what we constantly heard from our coaches, so that's what we believed. We were told that if we took a week off at this age—when normal girls are going through puberty—we might grow two inches and gain five pounds. Our sport is demanding because it's not possible to "play" gymnastics, like one can play basketball, football, or most other sports. You either *are* a gymnast or you *are not*. Gymnastics uses so many different muscles and motions that have to be consistently repeated or they'll just go away.

I could tell if I had taken a single day off. When I'm up on the bars, I have to have accuracy and precision. Even if I'm just a second off, I'm off . . . possibly dangerously so. That means I could fall off the beam or off the bars. A day spent recovering from an injury means I might have lost the skill to let go, flip, and then catch a bar. It only takes one time of missing the bar for disaster to strike. That's why gymnastics is so hard. We can't have an off-season or even an off day. We don't take long vacations and rarely take short ones. Gymnastics is—and must be—our life.

Twelve weeks off could mean the end of my career. Since the Olympic Trials were coming up in Philadelphia, I was particularly serious about not sitting in a cast at home.

"I'm going to get a second opinion," I told my doctor.

So I got a second opinion, and a third, and a fourth. Every single doctor wanted to cast it. Finally, I relented and went home in a gigantic, terrible cast. Every time I looked at it, I saw years of training going down the drain.

Within days I was back in my doctor's office.

"I want this off, please," I said sweetly. I was hoping he might not realize that it had been on only a week.

"Nice try," he said. "I want you to participate as much as anyone, but you have to realize that our bodies heal on their own schedule, not the Olympics' schedule. Your leg hasn't had time to properly heal."

"If you're not going to get this off me, I'm going to have my dad cut if off," I finally blurted out. "And he's going to be using power tools in the garage."

The doctor reluctantly agreed under one condition: that I promise to wear a boot and rest for a little bit. Though this was a minor injury, it sobered me. It had looked like an Olympics spot was right there for the taking. But again I was reminded of what a fickle sport gymnastics can be.

While I got over my injury and trained for what would be the most important competition of my life, many other exciting things were happening. First, I began doing promotions for the Games. Over a two-week period, I went to Atlanta for a photo shoot for Coca-Cola and to Los Angeles for an NBC promotional shoot before heading to Houston for a US national team training camp. Then, *ESPN The Magazine* contacted my agent. Since 1998, the magazine has created an annual life of what they call "NEXT athletes"—a group of talented, emerging athletes to watch in the year ahead. I'd been chosen as one of those athletes, and they wanted to do an interview and photo shoot with me at my house.

As soon as the reporter and photographer showed up at our door with their cameras and lights, we welcomed them into our home. The only problem was that the reporter was allergic to dogs . . . and our house is full of animals. After a few sneezing fits, we decided to shoot outside in the yard while Mom ran to the drugstore to get him some Benadryl. The photographer wanted to get a photo of me jumping. Of course, I didn't tell him I'd injured my shin. It was ESPN, after all. The photographer kept telling me, "Jump!" and then a few seconds later, "Jump!" Again and again and again.

Dad kept interrupting, asking me, "Shawn, is this hurting you?" It was, but I was so excited I wasn't going to tell the photographer. "I'm fine, Dad!" It felt as if I'd jumped a million times. The photos turned out great, though.

Constantly thinking about the Olympics could be nerve-racking, so I appreciated my "other life" more than ever. Though I still occasionally saw classmates pointing and whispering when I walked by, school helped me feel grounded and connected to my friends. Whether I was discussing Hemingway in English or dissecting a cow eyeball in biology, I felt a sense of freedom I didn't have when training so intensely. I loved hanging out with my friends too—strolling through the mall, going out to eat, or just laughing with them. I also enjoyed going out with Johnny, my high school crush. Because he sometimes pushed the rules, my friends and family weren't sure he'd be the best influence on someone like me. They didn't need to worry; he was kind and protective of me. If we went to a friend's house and someone brought out alcohol, he'd turn us right around and we'd leave. I appreciated him because he distracted me from the stress of competition and was a good friend to me during all of the chaos.

I kept trying to keep my gymnastics world and my school world separate, but it was getting increasingly difficult. That's why I resisted having any film crew come to my school. Several magazines requested permission to do that so they could get footage of me in my "normal life." Everyone thought it was novel that I actually attended school. Finally, *People* magazine was given permission to send a photographer to follow me around at Valley High School. Instead of the week the magazine wanted, though, the photographer was given just one hour.

That day I was nervous as I got ready for school, though I purposely wore the same type of clothes I'd usually wear. I warned my friends to act normal, but everyone was chattering with the excitement of having a film crew from *People* in our school. As I sat in English class, the photographers were outside waiting for the bell to ring. I'd been instructed to switch classes and walk slowly, greeting people in the hall as I went. That would provide some nice images of my non-gymnastics life. However, when the bell rang, I gathered my books and darted to my next class with my head down, not saying hello to anyone. The camera crew had to chase after me, and I felt ridiculous. By the time they found me in my next class, their allotted time was up, and they finally left!

Though I managed to avoid feeling completely in the spotlight that day, I felt just as embarrassed when I stumbled across a giant cutout of me not long after that. While picking up a few items at the local grocery store, I turned the corner of the aisle and spotted, just a few yards away, a life-size cardboard image of myself in front of a Coca-Cola display. I got out of there fast, wondering what shoppers would think if they saw me staring at myself.

Because I tend to be upbeat and love life, I knew that many people who saw that promotional cutout or read about me in their local paper assumed I never got anxious. Actually, I'm usually nervous before a competition—I think that's only human when you want to do your best. Rather than talking about all my deepest thoughts and emotions, though, I prefer to let them spill out in the lines of a poem. The pressure had really begun to mount by the spring of 2008, and so I often wrote down my thoughts in my journal. Sometimes as the lines came to me, I used my phone to text the words to myself so I wouldn't forget them.

While I was at a selection camp for the American Cup in March 2008, I was struggling to perform and was doing poorly on all my routines. After another rough day, Coach Chow pulled me aside and told me, "If you don't get your act together, I'm going to take you home." I knew he was right to call me out, but I had no idea how to fix my performance. I went back to my room and lay down on my bunk. I couldn't sleep, though, because all sorts of thoughts kept going through my mind. Finally, at 3 a.m. I got up, grabbed my phone, and typed my thoughts into a notebook app. Before long, the words began forming into a poem, which began this way:

> *You fear the loss and pain of defeat,*
> *but still are able to stand on two feet.*
> *You crumble and cry as much as you want,*
> *but nothing can keep you away from the hunt.*

I wrote for a full hour and finally lay back down and tried to get a few hours of sleep. The next morning, after I reread what I'd written, I realized a weight had lifted. Rather than being distracted by all kinds of conflicting feelings, I had sorted out my thoughts, my hopes, and my fears in the lines of a poem I called "Champion." After that, my performance turned around, and I was selected to go to the American Cup at Madison Square Garden.

While still at the Karolyi ranch, I sent the poem to my mom, telling her how perfectly it expressed my feelings. I'm often reluctant to share what I've written, and this time was no exception. Rather than telling her I wrote it, I asked her what she thought of this poem I'd found on the Internet. My mom texted back to say she loved it too.

In fact, as a surprise, she asked a local artist to paint the poem on a canvas. Then she hung it over my bed before I returned home. It was beautiful, and I finally admitted to my mom that I had written "Champion." Not long after, when a reporter from a TV network came to our house to do a profile on me, the interviewer heard about the poem and asked me to read it on camera.

While I felt a little strange reading "Champion" on air, it was probably the truest expression of my emotions as I looked ahead to the Olympic Trials. Part of the poem expressed my conflicted feelings:

You remember the times when you thought to give up
but could never find a reason to disrupt . . .
anything and everything that you had given to the sport,
the heart's desire and all the support.
But when the pressure builds and tears you apart,
how are you able to not depart?
How are you able to still carry a smile
when everything inside is in a pile?
You hold your head high and never look back
because this is what keeps you all intact.

Lesson I've Learned

Have patience. Learn to pick yourself up and push through hard times. Find an outlet that allows you to let your emotions run free and get rid of negative energy. That might mean talking with someone, running, watching a funny movie, or crying. Then you'll be able to begin the next day fresh.

CHAPTER 10

TRAVAILS AND TRIALS

Leap and the net will appear.
—*John Burroughs*

As my sophomore year was coming to an end, I listened to friends discuss their plans for the summer. Some were planning family vacations or looking for a summer job. Most talked about how they were looking forward to sleeping in and just hanging out at home. While their summers stretched before them like a peaceful stream, mine felt more like a raging river as I raced to prepare for the major competitions of my life—the Olympic Trials and, I hoped, the Olympic Games themselves.

I wanted to take part in at least one end-of-the-school-year tradition, though: prom. My parents were all for it. They thought the dance would provide a needed mental break from what lay ahead.

So in May, just a month before the Olympic Trials, Johnny and I, along with a big group of friends, went to prom. I had picked out a sparkly yellow dress that made me feel glamorous. Later, our group attended an after-party hosted by a group of parents at our local mall. After dancing and laughing the night away, I went with several of my girlfriends to a sleepover at one of their homes. When my friends and I got up a few hours later, we headed to Perkins for breakfast. It was just the break I needed.

About a month later, prom seemed like a distant memory. By this time Johnny and I had agreed to be just friends. I knew I'd never be able to keep our relationship going as I prepared for the rigors of the Olympic Trials.

One of the questions I'm asked most often is, "How is a gymnast chosen to participate in the Olympics?" There's no easy answer to that seemingly straightforward question. In other sports, the top qualifiers in the Olympic Trials automatically head to the Games, but that's not the case in gymnastics. Though we don't actually jump through hoops in our floor exercises, we figuratively jump through plenty of them for the honor of competing in the Olympics.

For me the first big test would come at the Visa Championships held in Boston. Though nationals are held annually, the competition during an Olympic year is particularly fierce because of one important fact: the top thirteen finishers move on to the Olympic Trials.

There were about fifty junior and senior competitors, and the excitement was high. Sponsors hosted exhibits for the audience to enjoy—CoverGirl set up an area where spectators could learn makeup tips; Tyson had an area to teach kids about fitness; and the entire 1988 US Women's Olympic Team was recognized to mark the twentieth anniversary of the Olympic Games in Seoul, South Korea. Outside the arena, women's gymnastics fans filled the city and flooded its shops, restaurants, and historical sites while they waited for us to begin. In other words, this was a big event, surrounded by hype and media attention.

The team for Beijing would be decided based on the results of the events in Boston, the Olympic Trials two weeks later in Philadelphia, and a selection camp in Houston in mid-July. Despite the pressure we all felt at the Visa Championships, I realized it wasn't a do-or-die event. I only needed to place in the top thirteen to go to the Trials, so I tried to think of it as a good time to get some more experience without overdoing it and risking injury. By this time my stress fracture had healed, but I had to stay healthy if I was going to make it to the Olympics in Beijing. I had a good day and won gold in the all-around for the second straight year.

I returned home with less than two weeks remaining before Trials. One day as I was getting ready to leave for practice, it was raining heavily. I looked outside and noticed large puddles accumulating in my backyard. The rain was coming down hard, but I didn't think much about it. I was thinking about—what else?—the Olympic Trials, which were now only one week away. I was trying to pump myself up for the important upcoming week of drills and practice.

I drove to practice in the rain, and when I left the gym, it was still pouring. I got in the car, turned my windshield wipers on to the highest speed, and marveled at how much water was coming down. I let myself into our house, made myself dinner, and watched some TV. My parents weren't home, and I was enjoying the solitude of the quiet, rainy night.

After a while, I glanced at the time. Eleven o'clock? It wasn't like my parents to stay out late and not call.

I flipped the channel to the news and heard the reporter mention a flood warning. Some businesses had announced that they would not be open the following day. Concerned, I dialed my dad's cell phone.

"Where are you guys?" I asked when my dad picked up.

"We're at the gym," he answered. "We're with Johnny and his friends."

"What? Why are you at the gym? And why is Johnny there?"

Though my parents liked Johnny a lot, they usually didn't hang out together. It still hadn't hit me that it might have something to do with the pouring rain.

"Shawn," he said, "we're here sandbagging. The river is rising."

I couldn't believe it. We had one week before Trials. And the gym was about to flood?

"I'll be right there," I said, reaching for my keys.

"No," Dad said quickly. "That's why we didn't call you before. Chow doesn't want you down here. The bags are fifty pounds each, and he doesn't want you to hurt yourself right before Trials. He wanted me to tell you to get some sleep."

It was just like Chow to worry more about me and the Olympic Trials than about his own gymnasium. It was also just like Chow to think I'd listen to him. There was no way I was staying home while my home-away-from-home flooded.

I got in my car and drove toward the gym, but the water was coming up so quickly that the police had decided to close the road and had set up a barricade to keep traffic off it.

When I got to the barricade, I rolled down my window. A police officer shone a light into my car. "Sorry," I said, "but I *have* to get to the gym."

The policeman recognized my face and realized what was at stake for me.

"All right, but be careful." They took down the barricade for me and wished me luck. The whole town was aware of the Olympics and how important the coming week of practice would be. When I got to the gym, the waters were still rising and getting close to the building. I couldn't even park in the parking lot.

I spotted Johnny and called out to him. He and his friends were lifting and placing sandbags like they weighed nothing. "Johnny," I yelled, "what are you doing here?"

"I'm not going to let a little thing like a flood keep you out of the Olympics."

I rolled up my sleeves and began helping too, though Chow wasn't happy about that. We ended up staying until two o'clock in the morning.

I went to sleep knowing that I probably shouldn't have stayed up so late or handled those sandbags. But I wasn't going to sit back and watch my gym be destroyed. I've never fallen asleep faster.

The next morning, I woke up around ten. When I looked at my phone, I saw I had missed numerous texts.

"Go to Chow's!" one read.

"Have you heard about the gym?" read another.

I jumped into the car and drove across town. I got as close as I could to the gym. The Raccoon River, a tributary of the Des Moines River, had flooded. Water was absolutely everywhere, and I half expected Noah to float by with a bunch of animals sticking their necks out of an ark. Several of my friends and teammates had already arrived at the gym in some canoes. In spite of all our work, the gym was four feet underwater.

Then it hit me: *I have nowhere to train.*

The Trials were one week away, and I had to be in the best shape of my life to make the team. Right then I seriously believed my Olympic dreams had been washed away with the waters that had destroyed nearly all of the equipment in the gym. I thought perhaps I could call Martha and get permission to train in Texas. I wanted to stay and help rebuild the gym, but first I had to get through the Olympic Trials.

Fortunately, I was invited to train at Iowa State University in Ames, which is about thirty minutes away from my home. Chow and Li went with me. Though it was far from the ideal situation, I was grateful to be closer to home. Then, just a couple of days later, my mom called.

"You can come back!" Mom said. "The gym is open!"

The entire community had banded together to rebuild it for us, realizing how much I stood to lose. When the water subsided enough to start rebuilding, that's what they did. The flooring had been so saturated that it moved when someone walked across it. It had been ripped out and replaced, thanks to a generous gift from my sponsor Coca-Cola. Several feet of drywall around the entire gym also had to be replaced. Destroyed mats and equipment had to be removed.

I will never forget the outpouring of generosity from my neighbors and community. They managed to put the gym back together before anything else in the neighborhood. (The house next door was still uninhabitable, but Chow's was up and running!) It seemed like everyone I knew had come out to help clean up the mess. Their acts of kindness allowed me to spend the last few days before we left for the Trials training at Chow's gym. The uneven bars and balance beam had been spared, and it was comforting to spend the day before the competition in familiar surroundings.

Throughout the ordeal, reporters kept calling, asking if I'd still be able to compete. It was like asking a fish if he was going to swim. Gymnastics was my life, and my hometown had given me a second chance to follow my dream to the Olympics.

A local company arranged to fly me on their private jet to the Olympic Trials, which would be held at the Wachovia Center in Philadelphia. It definitely took away some of the stress after the disaster we'd been through at home.

When I arrived at our hotel, I was basically on my own. My parents would fly up a few days later, but in the meantime, I walked into Center City alone to get my meals. Because my roommate had come down with a cold, I got my own room with a king-size bed. I loved the independence and freedom, and when I was with the other gymnasts, we chatted incessantly about the Olympics and about our fears and dreams.

After my practices, I read some books to help me focus on the task at hand: *Body Mind Mastery* by Dan Millman and *The Mental Edge* by Kenneth Baum. Reading helped keep me in the zone, which is exactly where I needed to be for the most important competition in my life up to that point.

Almost fourteen thousand people showed up to see the competition, which made it one of the largest audiences I'd ever competed in front of. Again, I didn't wilt under the pressure, though this was the most pressure I'd ever been under in my life.

I met the challenge and came in first in the all-around. Because of Nastia's and my first- and second-place finishes in Boston and Philadelphia, the media reported that both of us automatically qualified for the US Olympic Team. I was absolutely thrilled. The other girls who qualified to move on from the Trials would go to the selection camp at the Karolyi ranch, where Martha would evaluate all the aspiring Olympians using the scores from Boston and Philadelphia as a starting point. For three days, all of the girls would perform their best routines while Martha decided who would see their dreams dashed and who would go on to possible Olympic glory. Nastia and I would attend the camp as well, but we had already earned our places on the team.

I'd never spoken of the Olympics in concrete terms until that moment. I had hedged my bets and spoken in hopeful—not definite—terms. But finally, after all of the training I had done and my performance in Philadelphia, I could finally say, "I am an Olympic athlete." It was like a gigantic, oppressive weight had been sitting on my shoulders for years. And for the first time, it had lifted. I could breathe. I was going to China.

But first, the rest of the Olympic team would be determined in Texas, so I packed my leotards and headed to the ranch. However, as soon as I arrived there, I was surprised to learn that Nastia and I had been taken off the Olympic roster.

Nothing is ever certain. Not in our sport.

Lesson I've Learned

Surround yourself with people who care for and support you. Even when I lost hope, the loving people I'd surrounded myself with pushed me on to fulfill my dreams.

NOTHING IS CERTAIN

Waiting is not just something we have to do until we get what we want. Waiting is part of the process of becoming what God wants us to be.

—*John Ortberg*

"NOT SO FAST." That's what Martha seemed to be saying when she announced that we would *all* be competing for the six slots on the Olympic team. "That includes Nastia and Shawn," she emphasized. Who's on top in gymnastics can change with one slip off the beam, or one fever, or one miscalculation when trying to grab the bar. That's why the Olympic team isn't selected until the last possible moment.

Twelve girls arrived at the ranch with high hopes to make the Olympic women's gymnastics team. But this time, we weren't the only ones at the secluded ranch. It seemed like every publication, every media source, every sponsor, every parent, every family member had come to watch. Our team doctors were on edge because our bodies had been pushed to their limits; they were also afraid some of the girls' minds might be too overwhelmed by the pressure. Plus, they were worried about the moment when some of us would be told our dreams had come to an end. It felt like there was no oxygen in the entire place. Nobody was breathing. Nobody was talking. Nobody was interacting. Gymnasts were housed in the dorms, but everybody else was staying in hotels thirty minutes away.

On the first day, we performed our routines over and over in front of the coaches, the selection committee, about twelve members of the media, and some of Bela's friends, who had been invited to give their input.

On the second day, Mary Lou Retton showed up in the stands, but we didn't really get to interact with her at all. She was there both as an unofficial adviser to the staff and as a palpable reminder of what our futures might one day look like.

In the end, they led all twelve of us into the cafeteria. We were sitting down when Martha and the selection committee came in. They didn't want our parents or coaches in the room because that would have made the announcement even more emotional and heartbreaking.

"You're going, you're going, you're going, you're going, you're going, and you're going."

That was it. Our team now had six members. And one of them was me.

Next, Martha named the three team alternates.

After the announcement, Martha was crying, and I remember thinking she must have agonized over the final decision. When the team was announced, we hugged and cried. There weren't many words in that moment.

After all that drama, the rest of the team consisted of the following people, whose names and bios would soon be broadcast across the country. There was Nastia Liukin, who was nineteen years old. She was born in Russia, the daughter of Olympic gold medalist Valeri Liukin and Anna Kotchneva, a world champion in rhythmic gymnastics. With nine medals, Nastia had tied with Shannon Miller for having the most World Championship medals in the history of American gymnastics. At the time, she had one of the hardest bar routines in the world. The press talked a great deal about our rivalry because she frequently came in a close second to me in the competitions.

Chellsie Memmel was twenty at the time of the Olympics. Born and raised near Milwaukee, she was the 2005 All-Around World Champion, had placed third all-around at the 2008 Olympic Trials and nationals, and had won six world medals. She even had two skills in gymnastics named after her: a double turn with leg fully extended in a "Y" on floor and a piked barani on beam.

Alicia Sacramone was a Winchester, Massachusetts, native who attended Brown University. She was a seven-time medalist at the World Championships, as well as the 2005 World Champion for floor exercise. She was the oldest member of our team and fit naturally into a leadership role. Many times she offered advice and understanding when we got stressed out.

Samantha Peszek was a sixteen-year-old from McCordsville, Indiana, where she attended Cathedral High School. She had come in third in the all-around at the American Cup.

Bridget Sloan was sixteen. Born in Cincinnati, she was a strong competitor in all the events.

Three alternates, Jana Bieger, Ivana Hong, and Corrie Lothrop, were selected in case of injury or in case the coaches wanted to make a last-minute substitution. I was thrilled to hear that Coach Chow had been named head coach.

Though I'd officially made the team, I couldn't celebrate yet. For about thirty minutes, we huddled in the cafeteria and tried our best to comfort the brokenhearted. Instead of sending out a list of team members to the parents, friends, and press, the officials had us line up and march back into the gym. We would be a walking announcement to the anxious crowd, telling them who had made it and who had not.

The parents had been waiting for a long time in the stands, probably exchanging awkward chitchat, wondering if they'd see each other in Beijing. They were hoping, praying, and watching the door.

When it opened and we began to emerge, they eagerly scanned the line for their daughters' smiling faces. For several sets of parents, their daughters simply wouldn't appear.

"I'm proud to announce the 2008 United States Olympic Team," Martha said. There was clapping; there were silent, distant stares; there were tears. All at once, from my vantage point in the line, I saw the following emotions spread across the once-eager faces: surprise, relief, anguish, joy, grief, bitterness, and finally—resignation.

At the time, I was just ecstatic over being chosen. But as I look back, I'm a little haunted by the broken dreams. My friends had trained just as much as—and often more than—I had. They'd started when they were toddlers; they'd skipped vacations, public school, movies, football games, and family reunions. They'd made gymnastics their lives, and yet in one decisive moment, they'd learned they wouldn't achieve their loftiest goal. The moms and dads probably experienced their own kind of disappointment.

My parents, however, were crying in relief. Though my mom never really wanted me to be an Olympic athlete (she didn't enjoy watching me perform such dangerous moves), she was happy I'd achieved my goal. Plus, it was a great validation of all of their efforts, accommodations, and sacrifices. Their daughter had made the US Olympic Gymnastics Team.

As I hugged them, I realized I wouldn't see Mom or Dad again for quite some time. Now that I'd been named to the Olympic team, I was officially dedicated to the task at hand. I'd be traveling with the group directly to Beijing and would only be able to text or call my parents from my cell phone.

I had no idea what awaited me.

PART 2

Champion

You fear the loss and pain of defeat,
but still are able to stand on two feet.
You crumble and cry as much as you want,
but nothing can keep you away from the hunt.
This is what you've been working for,
the pride and honor as you take to the floor.
You remember the struggles and pain you had,
when all the good had turned to bad,
when behind the scenes you crumbled and prayed
for it all to simply just go away.
The doubt and regrets of what you went through
sometimes just made you want to give it to . . .
the next girl in line that gave it her all
but always seemed to carry a fall.
You remember the times when you thought to give up
but could never find a reason to disrupt . . .
anything and everything that you had given to the sport,
the heart's desire and all the support.
But when the pressure builds and tears you apart,
how are you able to not depart?
How are you able to still carry a smile
when everything inside is in a pile?

You hold your head high and never look back
because this is what keeps you all intact.
It's what runs in your veins, and it's the key to your heart.
And it's only the beginning, only a start.
It holds a future that could never be told,
one that can shine with the brightest of gold.
The sky is its limits, and with the moon as its guide,
as no one could ever predict how high
one could travel with the hard work put in . . .
to truly become a champion!

CHAPTER 12

HANDSTANDS AT 35,000 FEET

The most important thing in the Olympic Games is not winning but taking part; the essential thing in life is not conquering but fighting well.
—*Pierre de Coubertin, founder of the modern Olympic Games*

AS WE PULLED OUT of the Karolyi ranch to head to the airport for our flight to Beijing, we saw the sign we'd seen many times before: "Y'all Come Back." I realized with a pang of sadness that our team—just as it was then—probably wouldn't be back. A gymnast's career is very short, with just a few years of peak performance. Since the Olympics are held every four years, this would probably be the last time we'd all be together for national training. I swallowed back the tears and tried to think of those cockroaches to make it less painful.

"Look!" Alicia said, pointing out the window. Outside, several police cars waited with their blue lights flashing.

"A police escort?" I asked.

With the police leading the way, we were able to get to—and through—the airport more quickly. Before I knew it, we were boarding the plane.

"Please turn off all electronic devices," the flight attendant said as we settled into our seats. I texted my parents one last time: "I love you. Taking off." Then I settled in for the nearly twelve-hour flight.

Mom and Dad had already bought refundable airline tickets to Beijing and would be heading over in a couple of weeks. Though they never assumed I would make the Olympic Team, they definitely didn't want to miss the Games if I were there. To avoid paying the highest priced airfare later on, Mom had bought tickets she could cancel if I didn't make the team. I was so thankful that she wouldn't have to do that!

The plane we flew on was a double-decker, a first for me. Most of the passengers were headed to the Olympics. Every few hours, we were instructed to get up and stretch. That meant that suddenly a bunch of gymnasts were doing handstands in the aisles. All in all, the flight was a restful time to think about the upcoming competition and to dream about what the Olympic Village would be like.

When we landed, we sleepily got off the plane and walked through the airport, getting our first look at the country. Everything was written in Chinese, which was disorienting. When we were led down to get our luggage, chaos broke out.

Everyone was yelling, and there were Chinese reporters and media crews everywhere. That's when it dawned on me: Chow was a celebrity! As a former champion gymnast in Beijing, Chow had been very popular there before he'd left to make a new life for himself in America. It had been fourteen years since he'd been back to his homeland. He had no idea whether the Chinese would welcome him or resent him for coaching their competitors. In an instant, it became clear that they loved Chow and were proud of him.

Taken by surprise, he told the crowd of reporters, "We just landed; I don't want to talk about anything yet." When they told him they'd been waiting for four hours to meet our plane, he relented. They mobbed him, and it got even worse as we headed to the buses. Because they were so excited about Chow's return, more and more people started following us. I could tell they were going to cover our every move.

What I didn't fully realize was that they'd also been following me. Since I was Chow's student, they loved me, too! Anticipating my popularity in China, Chow had told me before we left for Beijing that he thought the media there would ask me my Chinese name. If they cannot pronounce your English name, he told me, they'll remember your Chinese one. He then gave me my own Chinese name, which translated into English is "Golden Flower." The Chinese, he told me, always refer to beautiful girls as flowers. Their warm greeting was very special to me because I felt loved by people who didn't even know me.

My first glimpse of the Olympic Village was beyond anything I could have imagined. The beautifully arranged village is like a city, except completely spotless. It was built specifically for the Olympics near the city's historic district, just south of the venues for the competitions. The village consisted of twenty-two 6-story buildings and twenty 9-story buildings, complete with everything we could possibly need: dining halls, an entertainment center, a recreational sports area (including pool tables, tennis and basketball courts, and a swimming pool), a library, a medical clinic, a fire station, banks, shops, coffee shops—even a McDonald's, which was the official restaurant for the Games.

Of course, the village was teeming with athletes. Most were in their twenties or thirties and looked big, muscular, and mature. Athletes were hanging out and getting to know each other, using charades to overcome the language barrier. Then we walked in.

When our group of nine girls walked in confidently, the other athletes noticed our arrival. Needless to say, we loved the attention—especially since some of it was from pretty fine-looking guys.

It was a little surreal to be in Beijing and to be known and celebrated. With a population of over 1.3 billion people, China has four times as many people as the United States . . . which means that it is slightly larger than Des Moines, too.

It took a while to get over jet lag and adjust to the climate, even as we practiced our routines and received massages and physical therapy. While the other athletes were allowed to hang out and explore the Olympic Village, our activities were strictly limited. When we weren't eating or at practice, we weren't even allowed to leave our rooms, so we downloaded TV shows, designed tattoos we promised to get after the Olympics were over, and passed around books. Sometimes we went out for media interviews, including fun ones with Meredith Vieira and Matt Lauer. They were welcome distractions from the pressures of Olympic preparation.

But we did manage to entertain ourselves, even with all the restrictions. Nastia and I were roommates, and we decorated the walls in our room with postcards from home and inspirational quotes. Our team was staying on the ninth floor, just one floor above where the US men's cycling team was staying. At night, our doors were closely watched, so we'd go out on the balcony and talk to the cyclists on the floor beneath us.

I enjoyed getting to know all of the guys, but I really hit it off with Taylor Phinney, a cyclist from Boulder, Colorado. He was dating someone back home, so he was off-limits for me. That didn't stop us from developing a good friendship, though. Nastia and I had a lot of fun talking to Taylor and his teammates. The boys thought it was kind of sad that we (or rather our coaches) closely watched what we ate, so they tossed us Snickers candy bars late at night.

While we spent our evenings chatting from the balcony like Olympic Rapunzels (without the long, golden hair), we spent our days training. Frequently, we got to catch glimpses of the other gymnastics teams coming to and from practice. We'd crane our necks, trying to check out the competition. When we finally got to see the

Chinese team, we were surprised at how small they were. Only one of them was even five feet tall, and their average weight, we later found out, was seventy-seven pounds. One of them was missing a baby tooth, and the permanent tooth had yet to appear! I wondered what kind of pressure they were under. What would it be like to carry the hopes of 1.3 billion people on your tiny shoulders?

Finally, three weeks after we left Texas, the night of the opening ceremonies arrived. In Chinese superstition, a day is considered lucky if it sounds like a word that has positive connotations. Apparently, the word for the number eight is *ba* in Mandarin and *paat* in Cantonese. Because these words sound similar to the words for prosperity (*fa* in Mandarin and *faat* in Cantonese), the opening ceremonies were held at eight minutes after eight o'clock in the evening on August 8, 2008. This date and time was believed to be the luckiest possible moment to start the Games. And—wow—what a way to start!

The event showcased China's rich history with jaw-dropping high-tech tricks and illusions during a four-hour extravaganza. It was produced by Zhang Yimou, a celebrated film director, and had more dramatic flair than any movie I've ever seen. After the parade of nations, the Olympic torch entered the stadium. Seven torchbearers carried it before passing it on to former Olympic gymnast Li Ning. He had been hoisted aloft by invisible wires and then "ran" along the rim of the stadium's roof carrying his torch. When he lit the enormous cauldron, thousands of fireworks lit up the night sky, officially beginning the 29th Olympiad. It was called the most impressive opening ceremony in the history of the modern Games, one that future hosting countries will be hard-pressed to match and that none of the 91,000 people in the stands watching will ever forget.

We weren't among them.

"The ceremonies are a just a distraction," Martha had told us. The gymnastics competitions began on the following day, and nothing was more important than staying in our rooms and preparing for them. Our team watched the ceremony on TV in our rooms. A few team members tried to downplay the opening ceremony, saying the events were overblown. However, I was glued to the TV, just as I had been when I watched the Olympics from the training center in Colorado Springs.

These opening ceremonies were even more amazing, such a nice representation of China's long history. As an American, it's hard to imagine that Beijing is over two thousand years old. After all, we think of a building that's 150 years old as "historic." Beijing is filled with historic sites that are many hundreds of years old. For example, Tiananmen Square, the site of several important events since its construction in the seventeenth century, is best known today as the place where the government cracked down on a pro-democracy movement in 1989 by declaring martial law and killing hundreds of protesters. The Palace Museum, where many emperors have lived, houses a collection of artifacts from over eight thousand years of Chinese history. Though we weren't there for a sightseeing adventure, I hoped that after our competitions I'd be able to join my parents and visit some of the sites with them.

By August 8, I was anxious for the Games to begin. My teammates and I were getting a little testy under the pressure and the constant training. Chellsie had broken her ankle while we were practicing before the Olympics, and her injury weighed on all of us. We worked hard to keep our spirits up, but it was tough. To make matters worse, I was homesick, which made me decide I wanted to be free of the sport that had consumed my life up until then. I wanted to set my own schedule, to work out in a regular gym like everyone else, and to start a different phase of life. With all of the injuries and heartbreak surrounding gymnastics, I hoped to get out of the sport while I was still healthy, happy, and full of life.

The days away from home had started to wear on me. I began to really miss my parents. I hadn't seen them for weeks, and even when I'd seen them at the selection camp, I didn't *really* get to spend time with them. Since I was feeling so depressed, I called them.

"Mom?" I said into the phone, fighting back the tears. "What are you doing?"

I tried to sound normal, but she could hear the emotion in my voice, which caused her own voice to crack a bit.

"Just planning out what to do once all of this is over," she said, trying to sound chipper. "Want to go shopping after the competition?"

"Sure, Mom."

Within seconds I was crying. Weeping. My call had only made my homesickness worse, and the pressure seemed to have taken its toll on me. Even though my parents had made it to China, they still seemed a thousand miles away. There was nothing they could do to alleviate the stress or to make it better like they used to do when I was a child. No Band-Aid could heal the way I felt.

So I prayed.

"Dear God," I wrote in my journal. "I'm just afraid of getting hurt. Not just physically, but more mentally. I feel like I've put too much of my heart into this. I feel I've done enough work to deserve it, though, and I want it more than anything. Amen."

Now, a few days later, the moment I'd waited for had finally come.

Lesson I've Learned

Sometimes the real victory comes from simply not giving up. Just remember: God is big enough to handle every challenge, and he is loving enough to calm every fear.

CHAPTER 13

THE SHOWDOWN

Life is mostly froth and bubble,
Two things stand like stone,
Kindness in another's trouble,
Courage in your own.
—*Adam Lindsay Gordon*

VICTORY IN GYMNASTICS often comes down to tenths of a point. That was certainly true during much of our face-off with the Chinese Olympic team. Though six other countries fielded teams in the all-around competition, everyone knew this matchup was really between the Chinese gymnasts—the 2006 world champions—and the United States team, which had taken the world title in Germany in 2007.

Even before we met the Chinese in the finals, my teammates and I knew taking the gold wouldn't be easy. Chellsie Memmel had broken her ankle in early August while practicing for the floor exercise. In an eerily similar mishap, Samantha Peszek sprained her ankle two days after the opening ceremonies while warming up for the floor exercise in the qualifiers.

Martha had to scramble to rework our team lineups. Samantha had been expected to compete in all four events in the qualifying rounds; now she and Chellsie would compete only on the uneven bars.

Watching Samantha go down after spraining her ankle had stunned the estimated fifteen thousand spectators and upset many on our team. After competing so often, though, I knew I had to control my thoughts and emotions by staying in my own little world. If I didn't ignore what I couldn't control, it would rattle me, too.

I made it through Sunday's qualifying round without any major errors. Our team looked especially strong on the balance beam. At the end of the competition that evening, all six of us gathered in a circle in front of the balance beam and put our arms around one another's shoulders. We were proud of making it through a difficult day.

Two days later, on August 12, we met the Chinese in the team final, one of the most anticipated events of the Games. The Chinese remembered what had happened at the 2007 World Championships, when we beat them by less than a point to win the team gold medal.

So far in Beijing, their routines had looked crisp and clean. They demonstrated masterful technique in their skills, and several of their routines had a higher level of difficulty than ours. On top of that, they were performing with a home-field advantage. This was their opportunity to prove and demonstrate their country's remarkable rise, a way to validate their way of life and their politics. China had spent a huge amount of money to impress everyone with their opening ceremonies. But they'd also spent a great deal to make sure they won more gold than any other country—especially the United States.

To add to the pressure, rumors and allegations about the age of some of the Chinese gymnasts were swirling. The *New York Times* had unearthed some Chinese sports registration lists that indicated some of the women gymnasts might not have been old enough to participate in the Olympics. When one reporter asked a tiny gymnast how she had celebrated her fifteenth birthday, she hesitated before saying it was just like any other day. The accusations created a heavy fog of bitterness and resentment around the competition . . . the one we were about to walk into.

Yet determining their eligibility was out of my hands, another issue I couldn't control and so didn't worry about. Besides, before the competition, when I'd meet the Chinese gymnasts in the Olympic Village, we would laugh and tease one another. Though we had to overcome the language barrier, we did that fairly easily by using sign language, smiles, and the occasional handstand.

As much as I admired the Chinese team, I had no mixed feelings when I walked into Beijing's National Indoor Stadium on August 12 for the team final. Eighteen thousand people were cheering as we took our place on the side, and I wanted nothing more than to beat their hometown favorite. I wanted to show the world that America was a powerhouse in gymnastics and that we'd come to compete.

No, this wasn't an individual competition. That would come a few days later. I'd come to the Olympics with a team, and as a team we were about to show the world what we could do.

Chow had told me just to be myself and not to try to do anything differently now that we were in Beijing. I kept his words in mind as I prepared for my first vault. In fact, our whole team started off strong, and after that first rotation, we were slightly ahead.

But when we got to the balance beam, things started to go wrong. For some unknown reason, Alicia, the first US gymnast on the balance beam, had to wait an unusually long time for the go-ahead to begin her routine. Finally, she was given the signal to start and began with a running start into a front flip. Much to our astonishment, she landed with her foot slightly off the beam, which left her teetering. Then she fell off. It all happened so fast that we almost couldn't believe our eyes.

By the time we got to the floor exercise, China was beating us by a whole point. On Alicia's second tumbling pass, she came out of a flip and fell backward. To make matters worse, Nastia and I stepped out of bounds during our floor exercises, infractions that cost us each a tenth of a point.

As our team captain, Alicia had rallied and encouraged us countless times; now it was my turn to encourage her. Once I'd finished my routine, I sat down next to Alicia, smiled at her, and took her arm in mine. The press assumed she apologized and I told her we all still loved her. That's not quite accurate. Actually, to get her to smile, I brought up an inside joke that had been circulating among our team. I wanted to keep her mind off what had just happened.

Meanwhile, the Chinese breezed through their routines to secure their first-ever team gold medal. The audience went crazy as the Chinese gymnasts hugged one another and smiled for the cameras.

Later, the press made a big deal out of the fact that the team didn't hold Alicia's falls against her and instead rallied around her. Of course we did. It's not like she planned to fall! Alicia wanted to go out there and win the gold as much as any of us, but it wasn't meant to be. As Chow had told me at Worlds, "Mistakes happen." We're human after all. The most important thing is how we handle our disappointments.

Not only that, but we had just gone from Olympic athletes to Olympic medal winners! Shortly after receiving our silver medals, Meredith Vieira interviewed us on *The Today Show*. Because my parents came to watch the taping, I finally had a chance to see them. They were in Beijing with their good friends Mark and Jill Oman and my agent, Sheryl Shade. I had a few, brief minutes to hug and talk with them. Seeing them made my emotions bubble to the top, but I had to get back to training. The individual all-around competition was only two days away, and I couldn't let the fact that I missed my parents affect the job I needed to do.

"Come on, girls," one of the coordinators said after the taping.

And so I hugged Mom and Dad one more time and swallowed hard. I hadn't seen them in weeks, and the ten minutes we had together seemed to make me feel worse, as if I were a thirsty person who'd been given a thimbleful of water.

Lesson I've Learned

Team members must never lose heart for one another. If you're part of a team, don't blame others or yourself for mistakes. Remember that when an individual stumbles, it is the team's mistake. Learn not to point fingers. God never abandons you and me, so why would we ever abandon our teammates?

CHAPTER 14

THE DAY I GREW UP

Those who trust in the LORD will find new strength.
They will soar high on wings like eagles. They will
run and not grow weary. They will walk and not faint.
—*Isaiah 40:31*

"WHAT DO YOU THINK?" I asked Alicia, holding up the gold ribbon I was thinking of putting in my hair. I was preparing for the individual all-around, the most prestigious and hard-fought Olympic gymnastics competition.

"Well, it's the *perfect* color," she said.

I laughed as I tied it in my hair and tried to calm my nerves. For months, the media had been speculating about my chances of bringing home four gold medals. I was determined to do my best in all my events, but I felt a pressure I'd never felt before as I got ready for this one.

By the time I walked into the arena, though, I felt exhilarated. I heard the crowd milling about, with the occasional eruption of cheers. Many people do worse under intense scrutiny, but I love the roaring crowds and the cameras. They invigorate me, and I seem to get an extra boost from the energy in the room.

Before performing, we're allowed to go through our routines in a warm-up gym, away from the area where the competition is going on. This allows gymnasts to really focus while going through their routines a couple of times. But that day, I couldn't tune out the crowd.

"Go, Shawn! Go, Shawn!"

I tried to think only about my vault, but the screaming got even more intense the more I ignored it. Mental alertness is very important on this apparatus since a gymnast literally hurls herself at a stationary object with all her might, then flips, sometimes without sight of the landing pad.

"Way to go, Shawn!" they yelled. "Go, Shawn!"

No matter how hard I tried, I could not tune out those voices. Though I didn't want to look into the crowds and get distracted, I finally decided it was too much to ignore. I scanned the crowd and saw a group of people waving like they were drowning and trying to get the attention of a lifeguard.

The entire Lopez family (who were at the Olympics to watch their son, Steve, compete in Tae Kwon Do), Coach Li, and my agent, Sheryl, were on their feet, cheering for me. It made my day and pumped me up. It was just what I needed to prepare for the individual all-around. I'd have to compete in four categories: vault, uneven bars, beam, and floor. The combined total of scores would determine the winner.

"All right, Shawn, you're about up," said Chow.

I knew it would be close between Nastia and me. The media couldn't get enough of her backstory, which played incessantly over the airwaves. Her father and coach, Valeri, was on the Soviet team that won gold in 1988; he also won a silver on the parallel bars, and another silver in the all-around. Her mom, Anna, was the 1987 world champion in clubs in rhythmic gymnastics. Nastia's story was one of a gymnastics legacy, and everyone wondered if she would be able to do what her father barely missed—win the gold in the Olympic all-around.

I had a similar story. Though I wasn't raised by gymnasts, I wanted to win this medal for my coach. He had been on the Chinese national team for twelve years, won more than thirty international medals, and was a national champion . . . in every event but the all-around. I thought it would be fitting if his protégé won that medal right there in his hometown.

But I wasn't thinking about any of that as I stood at the end of the runway waiting for the go-ahead for vault. When I saw my signal to go, I raised my arm to the judges and then ran down the runway. I did a round-off onto the springboard with my back to the vault. From the springboard, which was about four feet away, I leaped with my back arched and touched the horse for just a fraction of a second. Then, I pushed off enough to do a couple of twists before landing on my feet.

Chow helped me off the floor, and I went to go sit down while I waited for my score. I was smiling. One event down, three to go.

Bars were next, and I was ready for them. I saluted the judges, jumped up on the bars, and began my routine. As I performed, I caught the bar a little close, which scared me a bit. Sometimes it's easy to forget that the handstands and the elegant-looking bar routine can literally break your neck. However, when it came time for my big dismount, I absolutely nailed it.

"Yes!" Chow yelled as I raised my arms with a combination of pride and relief. I bounced up and down and heard the applause of the crowd.

I then moved on to the beam, my favorite event. I did a full twist, which I pulled off with a slight waver. The routine ended up being a great one, with a small step on my landing. Afterward, I hugged Chow as I climbed off the podium and went back to the sidelines to wait for the scores. That's when I felt compelled to look at the scoreboard—and nearly lost my breath once I realized I was out of the top three and a little over .6 of a point behind Nastia.

I turned to my coach and asked, "Chow, do I still have a chance to come out on top?"

He quietly led me to a corner of the arena and looked me in the eye. "Shawn, this isn't about fighting for the color of your medal. This is about demonstrating to the audience and the judges that you're the number one gymnast in the world. You need to pull yourself together." I let his words sink in as I walked up onto the podium to wait for the start of my floor routine. The way it works is simple. The gymnast watches a screen, which flashes the score of the previous competitor. Once her own name appears, she salutes the judges and begins.

As I stood waiting for Nastia's score to come up, I did the mathematical calculations in my head. I knew her difficulty level, I knew what score she normally received, and I knew what score I normally received. If she got no higher than a 15.2—which was a very normal score for her—then I still had a chance.

All I'd have to do was hit my routine, and I'd be on top. I'd been told a thousand times since we'd landed in China that "this was my moment." It's the biggest Olympic cliché, the most frequently repeated phrase an athlete hears once the Games begin. All of the endless training, missed vacations, and daily sacrifices were focused toward this one moment that I was just seconds from. My entire life's work had prepared me for this minute-and-a-half routine. I was ready.

Then, Nastia's score flashed up—a full seven-tenths of a point higher than the highest score I'd even conjured. My head began to spin with disbelief, because in that instant my dream died. I knew a gold all-around wasn't possible. There was no way for me to get a high enough score to win.

I look back at those seconds standing on the floor as the moment

I grew up. So many emotions, so many life lessons, so many sudden realizations were packed into a few, brief seconds. I stood there feeling more hurt than I'd ever felt in my life. I couldn't understand my low scores. I couldn't understand how I could have worked my entire life for something only to see it come down to this.

That was a tough spot to be in—one I hadn't counted on. I couldn't help but wonder, *Okay, do I just give up now? What's the point in going out there?* Then, for a split second, I looked over at my coach. He didn't look distressed; in fact, he stood with the same composure and calm facial expression I'd come to expect from him during these Games. When he gave me a small, reassuring nod, I could hear his voice in my mind: *If the gold medal is out of reach, go out and prove to yourself and the world that you deserved it.*

As I stood as one of the best in the world on a global stage in my coach's home country, it was his voice that echoed in my mind. "Finish what you start," he had told me a million times over the course of my life in his gym. His voice drowned out all of the other voices vying for attention in my sixteen-year-old head.

I was still determined to give this performance my entire heart and soul, but my motivation had changed. In some strange way, once I knew the gold was out of reach, I was free to go out there and just be me, the natural competitor who nonetheless had stuck with gymnastics since age three for the pure joy of the sport. I would show the world what I could do while having fun doing it.

I looked out into the stands, which were full of cheering spectators, and I thought of the millions of people all over the globe—in cities, in small towns, in rural villages—who were watching my floor routine on TV. I realized Chow was right. I would take to the floor knowing that, while I couldn't control how my rotations were scored, I could still win over the crowd and perform in a way that made me and my country proud. My nerves calmed as I realized that this was my moment to push through and to establish once and for all that I was the best female gymnast in the world.

"You're at the Olympics," I told myself, trying to get my head back into the game. "Enjoy this routine."

When I heard my music, I drew in a deep breath and took the floor. As I ran, the "there's nothing I can do" realization turned itself on its head. Instead of being oppressive, it was liberating! The weight of thirteen years of struggle, pent-up pressure, and work suddenly lifted.

As the music began, I felt complete joy. I did my first pass, and it was huge. I stuck that landing perfectly, as well as the landings on all the moves that followed. I did my leaps without even the slightest steps. I flawlessly performed a complicated move I'd added just that morning.

Adrenaline pumped through my veins as well as joy. But it was more than just the high of being able to pull off skills. It was the pride of picking myself up off the figurative mat and somehow being able to enjoy my moment. Everyone watching the routine knew I was no longer contending for the gold. Yet I could hear them clapping and cheering for me, which invigorated me even more. Even though I was doing a rather complicated, difficult routine, I never got tired. With every step, I felt energy surge through my body. I continued on with a nice double full, a great last pass, and then—remarkably— I had a perfect landing!

It was *the* greatest routine I'd ever done in my entire life. I stuck everything. As I finished my last pose, I was already bawling. I'd always wondered why so many people cried at the Olympics, but now I understood. So much emotion flooded through me. The crowd stood and applauded, and I was so grateful for their support.

I won, I told myself. It was a hard moment. While I may not have been awarded the gold medal, I'd won the hearts of the people watching. Once I'd decided I was no longer competing for a medal, I received the greatest reward ever.

I ran off the mat into Chow's arms, completely overwhelmed with emotion. I hugged Nastia's dad and some members of the Chinese team, and then I waited for the score.

15.525.

Nastia had won by more than six tenths of a point.

I was confused, happy, and upset as I searched the audience to find my parents. When I found them, sitting with the Omans, Sheryl, and Mary Lou, I noticed everyone was on their feet cheering for me.

"Way to go, Nastia," I said, giving her a big hug.

"We did it!" she said, and we cried over our first- and second-place finishes. It was the first time America had won gold and silver in the highly prized women's all-around. Actually, it was only the fourth time any nation had ever done so. We'd made history, and we were proud.

A little later, as I stepped up to the winners' podium to accept my silver medal, I realized that I wouldn't trade it for anything.

I'd won the all-around in the way that meant the most to me.

Lesson I've Learned

Learn to find pride in your own success, even if your accomplishment isn't recognized by others. Your worth isn't determined by the color of the ribbon around your neck or anything else someone might give you. God created you in his image; that is where your worth comes from.

CHAPTER 15

DO NOT MAKE
BOB COSTAS ANGRY

When a defining moment comes along, you
define the moment, or the moment defines you.
—*Kevin Costner*

"So, Shawn, how does it feel to lose?" the reporter asked, shoving
a microphone in my face. If that was not her exact wording, it's certainly what I took away from her question.

As soon as we walked off the floor, the media swarmed us.
America had made history by winning the gold and silver in
the women's all-around, and reporters were clamoring for some
quotes.

"I didn't lose," I said in disbelief. "I won the silver medal."

After being selected from thousands of gymnasts to represent
our country, I'd come in second among the world's best gymnasts.
Disappointed as I was, I knew I hadn't lost.

That moment was a rude awakening for me. I realized that, to
some people, the color of my medal really did determine my value.
Given the high expectations that had been placed on my shoulders,
perhaps that shouldn't have surprised me. But I knew the truth: I'd

managed to steel my nerves and dampen my disappointment before going out on the floor and giving the performance of my life.

In time, I came to understand that this silver medal was the most meaningful thing I took away from the Games. I had arrived in Beijing as a naive, innocent girl with stars in my eyes. Before long I realized how much was out of my control. My response to disappointments and setbacks, however, was completely up to me. If I'd gone into that floor routine knowing I had a lock on the gold, I'm not sure I would have performed it with as much freedom and joy.

Soon after the all-around, my mind was still surging with relief, disappointment, and pride—all at once.

"What was the worst moment of the Games for you?" another reporter asked me.

"I didn't have a worst moment—it's the Olympics, after all!"

I gave those interviews pretty mindlessly, my main goal being to escape the reporters' questions without bursting into tears. I largely managed it but became increasingly upset. "I gave my heart and soul out there," I said.

The reporter could tell I was about to cry, which—of course— made her simply press harder.

"Why are you so emotional?" she asked.

"I'm just happy to have been able to be here in the Olympics," I managed to say. Sensing an upcoming breakdown, my coaches mercifully yanked me from the reporters. They wanted to give me some time to process what had happened.

The Olympic Committee needed to be absolutely sure that we had not used drugs prior to the competition, so after our media interviews we went into a room for what we called "doping." We were closely watched as we provided a urine sample. I was so over-come with different emotions, though, that this indignity didn't even register.

As we left the drug testing room and prepared for more media interviews, I saw the other gymnasts being united with their families, and a surge of relief swept over me. It had been thirty-one days since I'd really seen my parents. The tears welled up inside me, ready to spill out once I could dive into their arms. But as I scanned the crowds, looking at all of the emotional reunions going on around me, my parents were nowhere to be seen.

"Have you seen my parents?" I asked one of the people who'd been ushering us from one place to another. I figured he would be able to help me find them.

"Oh, sure," the man said. "I know they're on their way."

I waited about half an hour.

"I think they should be here by now," I said.

"They're meeting us at the studio," he said. "I think."

Since Nastia's father coaches her, he had been able to join her immediately. Now I watched as other teammates enjoyed hugs and congratulations from their families. I tried not to wonder about my parents, but it soon became the only thing I could think about.

"Has anyone touched base with my mom or dad?" I asked. I couldn't reach them at any of the media stops and was getting frustrated that no one around me seemed to notice my plight. There was a lot of activity surrounding us. Shuttling so many people across this huge city in time for all of our appearances had to be a logistical nightmare. But the swirling chaos didn't lessen the pain of being alone. It just made it worse.

So I went from one place to another, smiling with my team and telling the world what a wonderful time I was having at the Olympics.

Our last interview was with Bob Costas at Beijing NBC. Mr. Costas had done a remarkable job of bringing the Olympic Games to American households, a very challenging task since there were so many sports to cover. It had gotten increasingly difficult for me to keep my emotions together as the hours passed without a word from my parents. But I tried to concentrate on the interview at hand.

"How did your parents react when you first saw them after winning the medal?" he asked after noticing the other gymnasts with their parents.

"I actually haven't had a chance to see them," I replied, hiding the pain under my cheerful-sounding answer. I thought I saw a flash of anger in his eyes even though we were on camera. Here I was, this young girl going through the most spiritually taxing moment of my life, and the organizers hadn't even bothered to help me find my mom and dad.

During the commercial break, he took me aside.

"Don't worry," he said very kindly. "I'll help you find your parents."

Within minutes, an NBC official called my agent and offered to send a driver to bring my parents and her to the studio. It was one of the most compassionate things anyone has ever done for me, and I'll never forget Costas's kindness.

As it turns out, my parents had been told after the competition to get on a bus headed back to the Olympic Village. By the time NBC tried to reunite us at its studio, I needed to go to the USA House with the other gymnasts for a reception in our honor. Once we arrived, the other gymnasts went directly into the reception room, while I went to another part of the house to wait for my parents.

Chow was already at the party, and he came over to talk with me. "You gave it your all," he said. "I wish there was something I could have done."

We replayed the competition, event by event, score by score.

"What else could I have done?" I asked, but I knew the answer. Eventually, resignation filled the room, and we just sat there in silence. Then, we heard a door open.

Finally, four and a half hours after the all-around competition, my parents were there. Chow jumped up and walked out to give us some privacy. There were no words, only sobbing.

"I love you," my mom cried. She was less upset over the silver than she was about how little she'd seen me over the past month. From the moment the Olympic Team had been introduced in early July, my parents had been nothing but spectators.

I had gone straight from camp to Beijing, where I was gone for five weeks. Of course, they had been in the stands, but in a very real way my parents had to sit on the outside and watch everything happen to me. They weren't able to be a part of it. They had to content themselves with watching from afar and smiling for the occasional camera shot.

At night, they'd sometimes get to talk to me on the phone, but those talks were less conversational than they were therapeutic. I called them weekly with another meltdown, when I'd cry into the phone and say things like, "I want to come home" or "I can't do this anymore" or "so-and-so is not being nice" or "I feel sick." It had to be terribly painful for them to realize I was going through so much for so long without being able to do one thing about it. Not a single thing.

But finally we were together again. And when I saw their faces, I realized it had been just as hard on them as it had been on me . . . maybe more so. Eight hours' worth of emotions—actually, thirteen years' worth—just flowed out. I'd come in second, but they were proud of me.

About fifteen minutes later, Sheryl came into the room. She told us that Peter Ueberroth, chairman of the US Olympic Committee, and Jim Scherr, the USOC's chief executive officer, wanted to meet us. The two men told me how proud they were of my performance and sportsmanship, saying I could not have represented the United States any better.

A few minutes later, my parents and I joined the reception downstairs. At last I was ready to celebrate. And in a way, though there were more competitions to come, right then I felt as if everything was over.

Lesson I've Learned

Your family members are the ones who will give your life joy and meaning. Remember that when you go home at the end of your day, your family will always be there.

CHAPTER 16

A TRULY WINNING BALANCE

Sports is human life in microcosm.
—*Howard Cosell*

"HEY! I just wanted you to know the whole town supports you, and I can be your bodyguard once you get home."

I smiled at the text from a friend in Iowa and put the phone on the little table on my balcony. Taylor was outside his room below me, and we were having one of our late-night balcony-to-balcony chats.

"Look at it this way," Taylor said. "You are one of the top two gymnasts in the entire world! You should be proud!"

By this time I was exhausted from a day filled with intense emotion and disappointment. I was no longer reeling from the day, just fatigued by it.

"I got you something," he said. A moment later, a Snickers bar landed on my balcony.

"Thanks, Taylor," I said, picking it up and unwrapping it. It tasted delicious, and this time I didn't even hide the wrapper.

Before I finally went to sleep that night, my phone buzzed with texts of amazing support, from friends both old and new. My fellow

Olympian Steve Lopez texted, "You looked so graceful and beautiful out there! I'm so happy my brothers and I got to witness poetry in motion! You were amazing."

Then, my phone buzzed with another text that really lifted my spirits. I didn't know Olympian Michelle Kwan, but she'd gotten my phone number from a mutual friend. She wrote, "Hi, Shawn! I just wanted to say everybody is so proud of you. People love you, not because of the color of your medals but because of your amazing attitude, great spirit, and kicking talent. Keep your head up high and smile. Everyone loves you."

That last one was particularly meaningful. Michelle is widely considered one of the greatest figure skaters of all time, and she won the silver medal in the 1998 Olympics.

There's someone who understands how I feel, I thought as I took some Tylenol PM, snuggled into my bed, and turned out the light. *Maybe the only one.*

I was happy to put this day to rest.

A few days later, an article written about my time in Beijing began by pointing out that while I had been favored to win several gold medals at the Olympics, I still had not earned a single gold. *Thanks for the reminder*, I thought.

Next up, after the team competition and the individual all-around, I faced the floor exercise finals. For the third time in the past five days, there was a gold medal at stake.

Wearing a midnight-blue leotard with a white ribbon holding back my hair, I was first in the lineup to compete at the National Indoor Stadium. Expectations for me were high since I was the reigning world champion in the floor exercise. I landed my first run perfectly, and the crowd loved it. While I performed, people called out my name in encouragement, and I delivered what the announcers called a very compact and controlled performance. Since I was the first to perform, my 15.5 was the score to beat.

Would it be enough for that much-coveted gold? I watched from the sidelines, pretty content since I knew I'd given it my all.

All the gymnasts did a great job, but I held on to the lead all the way until the end. Then I watched as Romanian Sandra Izbasa started her routine. Since she began with a higher degree of difficulty than anyone else, she could quite possibly take the gold. From the side, I watched her hit every tumbling pass with a solid, unwavering thud. By the time her routine was over, the gold medal had slipped away from me.

Of course, when you're training your whole life to get to the Olympics, you train for gold. But a silver medal around my neck three times at the Olympics was still pretty impressive. At least that's what I told the reporters. Honestly, I was disappointed that I hadn't won a gold medal. I felt like I'd let down many people who'd believed in me.

Strangely, though, I was beginning to feel a little dulled by the whole experience. It had been a long road, and since I'd done my best, I just kept looking ahead. Even the *New York Times* reported that I seemed "markedly less stunned than she had on Friday after the all-around."[3]

Everything seemed different after those eleven seconds on the mat before the all-around. I realized that gymnastics was no longer the most important thing to me, and that I'd essentially already won. I knew that my friends and family loved me, that God was watching over me, and that I had represented my nation well at the Olympics. All in all, I knew that my life was solid and balanced.

On August 25, I had one more chance for gold: the balance beam finals.

I looked in the mirror after putting on my red-and-blue leotard accented with rhinestones. Now I just needed to decide which ribbon to tie into my hair. I found a Beijing ribbon from the award bouquet I'd received the night before. I smiled as I looped it around my ponytail.

This is it, I thought, trying desperately to rev up my competitive nature. *I came to win a gold, and I've got one more shot.*

But during warm-ups in the back gym, my confidence completely disappeared. I could tell I simply wasn't "on." When you start training so many years in advance of a big competition like this one, you sometimes wonder how your performance will go, whether it will be tainted by sickness, injury, or other circumstances beyond your control.

Even worse, however, is when nothing is wrong at all . . . when you're simply not able to pull off a routine you've done a million times. At least if you have a broken bone, you have some tangible reason that explains away an imperfect routine. And perfection is what we aim for. In other sports, athletes strive for excellence. In gymnastics, we strive for perfection.

Chow looked at me with concern when he first saw me at the arena. He started encouraging me and even got me into warm-up about forty-five minutes earlier than normal. After some conditioning, I mounted the beam with a springboard to run through the routine, but I immediately started feeling heavy and tired. This, of course, was not a good sign. Neither was the headache that simply would not go away and that got worse when Chow began to yell at me.

"You're taking too long!"

"Okay," I said, trying to get into a steadier, faster rhythm. I knew he was right. So I sped up my performance, but doing so threw me off-kilter. I swung my arms up in an effort to steady myself, but the correction was not enough. I fell. Since the beam is only four inches wide, falling might be somewhat understandable . . . if I wasn't favored to win a gold medal in this competition. As it was, the people who were watching me gasped in amazement as I fell four feet and hit the floor with a thud.

Chow ran his hand over his face as I jumped back up on the

beam and suddenly—without warning—started flailing again. My arms were like windmills, trying to keep me on the beam, but I couldn't maintain my balance. *Smack!* Once again, I was on the floor.

By this time, the media, coaches, and some of my competitors had gathered to watch me run through my routine. Normally, gymnasts simply go through the motions as they practice their routines in the warm-up gym before a competition. We never go all-out because we want to reserve our energy for the real deal. Chow, however, was so furious at me that he didn't care if he might be exhausting me.

"I'm not even letting you perform unless you show me you can do this!"

He bit his lower lip in an effort to quell his anger.

I went up on the beam repeatedly, much to the surprise of the people watching. They seemed shocked at how many times I got up and how many times I fell off. I was falling apart before their very eyes. The beam was supposed to be my best apparatus, but I could barely even stay on it.

Time was running out. My stomach ached. I felt like I was in a fog. I jumped up but fell off again. Beam can be dangerous, too, if your heart and mind are not completely focused on your moves. Because it requires such extreme concentration, one distraction, one fearful thought can mean a face-plant on the beam or a perilous tumble to the floor.

Chow pulled me aside. "You're not going out there until you go through your routine without falling." What would people say if my coach didn't let me compete on my best apparatus in the Olympics? I searched his eyes and face and could tell that he absolutely meant it.

I mounted the beam quickly. The other gymnasts were completing their routines, one after another, as I continued to warm up. I was the sixth competitor of eight, and I could already hear the third competitor performing.

As I've mentioned, pressure normally doesn't bother me. I generally thrive under the intensity; somehow it pushes me to perform better than I would in a quiet gym alone. Not this time.

And it wasn't because I felt the pressure of the Olympics weighing down on me. Rather, I felt empty. I felt done. I'd come to the Games as a favorite to win the gold, but I was going to end up with a few silvers. *Not bad*, I thought. My face had already been on McDonald's bags and Coke cans, after all. Someone had even carved a life-size butter sculpture of me at the Iowa State Fair! It seemed everyone expected me to bring home a gold, but my chances to do that had dissipated into this one final opportunity.

"Do it again!" Chow said to me after I fell yet again. I could hear the fourth competitor preparing for her routine. I was competing against Nastia, who was the reigning balance beam world champion, and Chinese gymnast Li Shanshan, who had taken the silver at Worlds the previous year. Could I go up against them while I was in this kind of unfocused state?

"You came into this a favorite to win several golds. You haven't done that," Chow said. "This is your chance. Wake up!"

Finally, his words registered within me. If I wasn't going to show any passion about my performance, he would. I was having a tough time getting my mind back into the game after the all-around. Just as overconfidence can lead to unwarranted bravado, disappointment can lead to debilitating despair. In gymnastics, as in life, balance is hard to come by. But I was determined to try to find it.

On about my eighth attempt, I managed to go through the motions of a routine without screwing up too badly. It wasn't even that great, but Chow nodded at me. I'd managed not to fall, and he was letting me compete.

"Now you don't have to worry about the results," he told me just before I went out. "You need to go out there and do your best. And enjoy yourself."

I was able to catch the end of the Chinese gymnast Li's routine. She was considered the best in the world, and she began her routine well. Then she stumbled. During a full twisting back handspring, she lost her balance and began to fall to the floor. She tried to grasp at the beam to stay on, but she slipped off. This was an automatic eight-tenths of a point deduction, which put her out of reach of a medal. When the judges scored her otherwise amazing performance, she'd made a 15.3. She leaned against a wall as she heard her score. Tears filled her eyes.

When I walked out to the beam, I had no idea what was going to happen. With my usual confidence shaken, I realized I wasn't sure about anything anymore.

I mounted the beam, and I don't remember anything after that. Usually I talk to myself, reciting little reminders about what I should do and how I should concentrate. Not that night. It was like I was a little robot, allowing my muscle memory to kick in. I didn't even smile.

Before I even realized I had performed, I landed the dismount, with just a small step. Though normally I'm pretty accurate in my scoring capabilities, I couldn't predict how these Olympic judges would score my routine. In my mind, I figured I would get a 15.8. When my score was revealed, I was astonished.

16.225!

Although I now had the top score, I expected to watch my gold medal be taken away by another gymnast who was able to do her routine in a slightly more daring or more dazzling way. And so I positioned myself on the sidelines with a smile on my face. I'd managed to get through the disappointment pretty graciously so far, and tonight would be no different.

By the time Nastia performed, I had a feeling that Team USA was going to do it again! This felt oddly familiar, with the two of us battling it out for the top-place finishes. Who would go home with the gold? The commentators who narrated the battle of the balance beam said it was Nastia's grace and beauty versus my energy and power. And it was true—we did have different styles on the beam, on the floor, and in life. The differences were pronounced, and sometimes it came down to which style the judges preferred.

After her elegant beam routine, I hugged her. Would we do it again?

After a few tense moments, Nastia's score appeared: 16.025.

I was still in position to win the gold! Chow embraced me, but a gymnast from Japan still had to perform. After she went through her routine, it became obvious that I'd won the gold and Nastia had won the silver.

Bela leapt up and down in the stands and shouted while Martha pumped her arms in celebration. The United States had come in first and second! Our wins meant that we'd earned two more medals than the Chinese gymnastics team. And even though I had grown to appreciate my new Chinese pals, it felt great to win. Most gratifying of all was knowing that I'd given Coach Chow a gold medal in his hometown of Beijing.

I'd finally won my individual gold, earning the title of Olympic champion on the last event of my 2008 Olympic career. That's what you call cutting it close.

In a way, it was oddly anticlimactic. There was something about losing the all-around, which I had felt I was going to win, that was very clarifying for me. Don't get me wrong. I was honored to have won the gold in the balance beam competition—and relieved not to have fallen short of the expectations people had for me.

Yet over the past ten days I had been through the highest of highs and the lowest of lows. I felt as if a year of my life had been wrapped into those five weeks in Beijing. Truly nothing is more amazing than standing on the Olympic medal podium as "The Star-Spangled Banner" plays. But I realized then as never before that life is more than medals, perfect dismounts, and high scores. I'd worked on the balance beam almost my entire life, but I was only beginning to find a truly winning balance.

Lesson I've Learned

I enjoyed the glitz and glamour that came after winning the gold, but strange as it may sound, receiving my silver medals was just as gratifying. After accepting those, I better understood the meaning of this verse: "He gives us even more grace. . . . As the Scriptures say, 'God opposes the proud but favors the humble'" (James 4:6).

CHAPTER 17

MORE THAN
I'D BARGAINED FOR

All journeys have secret destinations of which the traveler is unaware.
—*Martin Buber*

AFTER OUR COMPETITIONS were over, I felt as if the lid had been lifted from the pressure cooker I'd been living in. The built-up stress from years of work poured into the ultimate competition had finally dissipated. Now I was free to enjoy the rest of the Games and our host country of China. I even got to enjoy it a bit more than the other gymnasts because of Chow—or Qiao Liang as he was still known in Beijing.

"You're not going to believe this," Sheryl told me. "You've been invited to be a guest on China Central Television." As the major state TV broadcaster in mainland China, China Central Television includes a network of nineteen channels broadcasting to over one *billion* viewers.

"You want to do it?" she asked.

"Definitely!" I said, without hesitation.

The interview was one of the most memorable experiences of

123

my life. The Chinese women's gymnastics team was seated right in the front of the audience, and they clapped enthusiastically when I came out.

A lot of that connection was due to Chow. Just by honoring me with the special Chinese name "Golden Flower," he had helped endear me to the country. It was so gratifying to see Chow return to Beijing as the head coach of an Olympic team. Even better, he came back as the coach of an Olympic champion. Appearing on China Central Television seemed like the perfect way to celebrate our success!

The producers played scenes from the Olympic Games on a giant movie screen while the host asked me about my life back home in Iowa, showed the viewers some drawings I had done, and even translated some of my poetry into Chinese. Chow graciously translated all of my responses, which was a lot of fun for me. As you can imagine, I didn't get to hear him speak Chinese too often when we were in Iowa. I also made a point to say that I believed the Chinese team deserved to win their gold medals. The crowd applauded when they heard that, of course.

The show's host presented me with some rather extravagant gifts—a jade pendant, a crystal plaque, and an enormous framed photograph of me from the Beijing Games. It was so gigantic that my mom discovered it would cost $700 to ship it to America. Fortunately, we realized that one of my sponsors could slip it into one of their bags and take it all the way to Des Moines for us.

At the end of the segment, I was asked to imprint my hand into a golden star, which was added to a wall of fame on the set. This is a privilege normally reserved for the most famous stars in China, so I was humbled and honored by this request. At the same time, appearing on that show was somewhat strange, since I didn't understand a word my hosts said. I felt much more comfortable when I was finally back at the Village relaxing with some of my new friends.

"No more balcony-to-balcony chats," I texted Taylor. Now that the gymnastics competitions were over, the coaches didn't care how many Snickers bars we ate or how late we stayed up.

Taylor invited me to hang out with him and his roommates soon after. Visiting in person was a lot more fun . . . and a lot more painful! "Catch!" Taylor said, whipping a gummy bear at me. It pelted me in the stomach and fell to the ground.

"Thanks a lot," I said, picking it up and hurling it toward his head.

He smiled as he swiped more candies out of the jar, like a bear getting honey. The other cyclists got in on the action too, and suddenly gummy bears were flying through the air like bullets in a war zone.

"Watch out!" I yelled at the guys as my legs got nailed with the candy. *Never get into a gummy bear fight with Olympic athletes*, I thought as I ducked behind a couch pillow.

When it was all said and done, I actually had a few bruises on my legs and a stomach full of gummy bears. I also had to admit to myself that I had feelings for Taylor.

Looking back, I understand why that was. It's hard to overstate the intensity of the Olympic Games. Taylor and I had gone through that experience together, and I'll always be thankful that I have a friend who understands what it was like. I sometimes wondered if anyone else could really "get" what we went through during those days in the beautiful Olympic Village. Since Taylor had a girlfriend back home, though, I had to be content with the fact that we were just friends.

On our last night there, Taylor came over and we talked for what seemed like forever. The next day I'd transfer to a hotel with my family since everyone else on my team was going home. No one was staying for the duration of the Games, either because of the expense or due to scheduling issues. However, my parents had decided that we would stay until after the closing ceremonies. After all, I'd missed the opening ceremonies, and how many opportunities do people get to be part of such a momentous event?

Before I headed out, Taylor picked me up in a long embrace, and my heart was heavy with the knowledge that there would be no more late-night chats with him and his buddies.

Booking a hotel room in Beijing during the Olympics was nearly impossible, but my sponsor Coca-Cola knew of my desire to stay for the closing ceremonies and provided accommodations for me, my parents, and Sheryl during the final days of the Games. St. Regis, our hotel, was in a prime location near Beijing's historical district, so we were able to visit many of the city's most famous sites.

"Check this out," my mom said as we put our luggage into the new hotel room. It was wonderful to see my parents so much and finally be able to just enjoy the country. "What a great room!"

It was pretty sweet. Since Chinese hotel rooms have either two twin beds or one full-size bed, Sheryl and I were sharing a room with two twin-size beds, and Mom and Dad were sharing another room with a full bed. Our room was beautiful, with an elegant marble bathroom. Plus, the hotel had a great international buffet with a large assortment of food. It was a big change from the Olympic Village. I plopped down on the sofa and turned on the TV to see if we could catch some of the other competitions.

"Oh, look," I said, pointing to the screen. "Martha's being interviewed."

My mom and dad settled into the couch next to me, and we listened as the interviewer asked her how she had met me. We were intrigued—we'd never heard this story from her perspective. We only knew that Chow had sent the videos he'd recorded in his gym to Martha with a note suggesting that she take a look at me. But Martha described opening the envelope from Chow postmarked West Des Moines, Iowa. She explained that he'd sent the video and attached a note that read something like, "Martha, you'd be stupid not to take this talented girl."

We laughed. Chow must have really believed in me. I mean, she's *Martha Karolyi*. People don't speak to her like that.

She laughed as she recalled thinking this coach must have guts of steel to approach her that way. Then when I came to their camp, she said I acted like I belonged there. "I thought, *Well, the man is right. She's got it*," Martha said.

I thought about how far I'd come since the day Chow had sent her that secret video. It reminded me that I never could have made this journey without Chow, and I was so thankful once again that he'd opened his gym in my little town.

"All right, guys," Mom said, refusing to go down any more emotional roads. "We said we wanted to go shopping. Who's ready?"

The Silk Market, a large, four-story building filled with booths selling clothing, handbags, shoes, and other items, was about a fifteen-minute walk from the hotel.

I grabbed my purse and headed out the door. I wanted nothing more than to go shopping so I could try out my bargaining skills. In Beijing, merchants expect you to haggle, which can be very hard for Americans to get used to. I'd been warned that the initial price offered by the seller—especially in these backstreet markets—is usually at least 40 percent over the generally acceptable price. Sometimes the price can be inflated by up to 500 percent.

The shops were crowded, and the merchants' idea of a dressing room was holding up a towel so you could try something on. Not my idea of privacy, but after drug testing, I guess I had lost some of my inhibitions. When I tried on my jeans, a saleslady smacked me on my rear and said, "Look at that cute butt!"

Very different from picking up jeans at the Gap.

"How much?" I asked a merchant, holding up the four pairs of jeans I'd settled on.

He held up a huge calculator and began tapping into the machine. "Four hundred each," he responded.

I smiled at him. "Really? No thanks."

As I was putting the jeans back on the table, he stopped me. "How much you pay?"

Since there was a language barrier, I used the only word I thought he'd know.

"Cheaper!" I said, smiling.

"Three hundred," he said.

"Forty."

"Forty?" he said in mock exasperation. "No, no, no," he said, holding up the jeans. "These are high quality. Not knockoffs."

"How much?" I smiled, realizing I had the "sweet, innocent little girl" look going for me. I fully intended to utilize that.

"Two hundred," he said.

I laughed and replied, "Forty-five."

"Okay, okay," he said, deleting the last number off of his calculator. "Last price: 160."

"Last price," I said, "eighty."

"No, these are good pants," he said. "These are one hundred or no profit."

"Okay." I put them back on the table and began to walk away.

"Wait," he said. "Okay, you want?"

I nodded, still smiling.

"Eighty-five it is."

I was able to score four pairs of jeans for a lot less than what I'd pay in America on even one pair of this brand . . . pretty respectable for a beginner. I stuck my jeans into a bag and went to the next booth.

Everything was going well until we tried to buy purses. I knew what I wanted but couldn't find any in the shops. One salesperson eyed me.

Growing Up in Iowa

Me at one and a half years old

Going to a junior high school dance

I could make a balance beam out of anything.

Team of Champions

Competing in the individual all-around at the World Gymnastics Championships in 2007

The Worlds team on NBC's *Today*

Off to Beijing

Outside the Olympic Village in Beijing

At NBC's studio in Beijing with my parents

Me and Chow after a competition

Giving It My All

Performing in the individual all-around

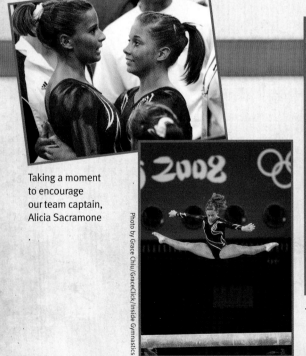

Taking a moment
to encourage
our team captain,
Alicia Sacramone

Photo by Grace Chiu/GraceClick/Inside Gymnastics

The beam routine was my last chance
to win a gold medal at the 2008
Olympic Games . . .

. . . and I did it!

Olympic Highlights

The Olympic medal–winning USA team!

Me and Li celebrating the gold medal win

Backstage at NBC with three people who made the Olympics special for me: Bela Karolyi, Chow, and Bob Costas

Celebrating with a Coca-Cola. (This was the only picture taken of me at the Games with all four medals!)

Wearing my first Olympic silver medal . . . with my parents; my agent, Sheryl; and my good friend and supporter Meredith Vieira

Special Moments

Leading the Pledge of Allegiance at the 2008 Democratic National Convention

On the red carpet at the *Hannah Montana* movie premiere in my cheerful yellow dress

Backstage at *The Ellen DeGeneres Show*, with my cousin Tori and Mario Lopez

Prom night!

Dancing with the Stars

Dancing the samba with Mark Ballas on *Dancing with the Stars*

Holding the famous mirror ball trophy!

Only the Beginning

Meeting a young fan

Looking toward the future . . .
excited to see what it holds

"You like?" a salesman asked.

The purse I'd picked up looked cheap. "No," I said, putting the purse down. I didn't want to accidentally get into a negotiation. All of the back-and-forth was a little exhausting, and I only wanted to engage in it if I really wanted an item.

"Follow me," he said, motioning to my parents, Sheryl, and me.

We all looked at each other and shrugged. Maybe this is how they do it, keeping the really good purses in the back for serious shoppers. We followed the salesman down a hallway into a separate room. It was actually a storage room with dead bolts on the door, probably to protect their stash.

The tiny room was filled with purses. There were a few other merchants in the room, and we felt outnumbered.

"You like?" one of the women asked.

"No," I said, smiling. I'd learned that smiling really helps when there's a language barrier.

"How much?" she asked.

"No thanks," Dad said, moving toward the door.

Leaving without a purchase didn't prove to be as easy as we'd expected. They started yelling at us in Chinese. Though I couldn't understand them, I figured they were probably saying something about us wasting their time, or about how stupid Americans are. Either way, they were going to make this as difficult as possible.

Mom's face turned red, and I could tell she was getting upset. The small room suddenly began to feel even smaller.

I shoved past the emotional saleslady, and everyone followed me out of the room and through the series of dead-bolted doors. I made it through one, but got stuck on the next.

"Dad, it's locked," I said, trying to control the panic in my voice.

The salespeople showed no signs of letting us out. By this time Mom was freaking out, Dad was yelling, and my agent was negotiating. I didn't think we were going to get out of there with our lives. Finally we got through the locks and back into the open air. We had that shaky feeling that comes when you've just avoided a serious car accident.

"Want to call it quits for today?" Dad asked. Too unsettled to continue shopping, we went back to our hotel with my jeans and our lives.

That night I got a call from Taylor.

"Would you like to go to an Oakley party with me?"

Oakley was his corporate sponsor, and the evening sounded like a fun outing. My parents, though, were not convinced that I should be going out with a nineteen-year-old.

"Come on, Dad," I protested, after telling Taylor I'd have to call him back. "He's dating someone else."

"Mom," I turned my attention to her when it looked like Dad wasn't budging. "How frequently are we in China with friends?" I emphasized the word *friends*, but she wasn't buying it.

My advantage that day was my agent, Sheryl. She also represented Taylor and knew he was a nice guy from a good family. Over the next hour, she showed off her negotiating skills, and my parents finally relented.

"I can go!" I texted Taylor and began looking forward to the party. I was not disappointed. The Oakley execs were kind to me and really welcomed me into their little family. There was music and dancing, but mostly I enjoyed hanging out with Taylor again.

"Hey, you want to dance?" a slightly drunk guy asked me, trying to pull me out onto the dance floor. I definitely had no desire to dance with him, but I loved seeing a flicker of anger cross Taylor's face as the guy tried to flirt with me.

"Leave her alone," he said to the guy. "Go on."

We were out really late. As I walked into my hotel, my head swirling with all of the fun I'd had, I was surprised to see my mom asleep in the lobby. I almost hated to wake her up, but I thought it was so sweet that she'd tried to stay up to wait for me.

The next morning, it was time for some good bonding time between Dad and me. I almost couldn't remember the last time I'd been able to hang out with just him. We began with an honest-to-goodness breakfast. Now that my Olympic competitions were over, I wasn't going to simply grab a banana. I ordered waffles and savored every syrupy bite, feeling like a kid again.

"Are you ready to *really* see China?" Dad asked, after I'd scraped the last bit of waffle off my plate. We decided to go to the Great Wall of China, one of the Seven Wonders of the World. The wall snakes its way through the mountains of northern China and is the longest man-made structure ever built. In all, it covers more than five thousand miles—twice the distance between New York and Los Angeles.

"Look, Dad!" I said as I did a handstand on the wall while onlookers took photos. People recognized me from the Olympics, and I felt almost giddy now that the pressure of the Games had been lifted. After posing for some photos, I put my "camouflage"— my hat and sunglasses—back on and walked with my dad. I was shocked at how my leg muscles were burning. You'd think an Olympic athlete would be able to handle walking on the Great Wall of China with no sweat, but that wall was steep!

At one point we rode gondolas to a certain part of the Great Wall.

When we decided to descend the wall, my dad brought up two options: "So, if we go right, we walk back down to the buses," Dad explained. "If we go left, we can toboggan down."

Of course, we chose those toboggans! Sleds were placed in a winding metal track, which snaked all the way down. I was thankful to have this option, since my legs had begun to feel like noodles.

"You first," my dad said, motioning to the first toboggan that became available. I got into it, put on my seat belt, and headed off like a slow-motion roller coaster. Well, it started off slow, but then it got fast . . . possibly too fast! The operator kept yelling in Chinese to slow down, but I wasn't really sure how.

Oh well. It wasn't the first time a Chinese man had yelled at me.

Lesson I've Learned

Seize the moment. You are presented with opportunities for a reason. Be sure to take and run with them.

CHAPTER 18

LAST NIGHT IN BEIJING

Friends are angels who lift us up to our feet when
our own wings have trouble remembering how to fly.
—*Unknown*

THE PHONE RANG in the hotel room Sheryl and I were sharing, and
she groggily reached over to answer it.

"Hello?" she asked, looking at the clock. Who was calling at
three o'clock in the morning?

"Sheryl," my mom's tired voice came through the phone. "This
is Teri. Is Shawn in her bed?"

Sheryl sat up and looked across our room at the twin bed that
was supposed to be mine. The comforter hadn't even been turned
down.

I'd gone out several hours earlier for one last evening with my
friends. I couldn't believe it, but we were flying home the next
day. I'd anticipated the Olympics for so long. We'd trained for
years, come to Beijing weeks before the Games began, and stayed
throughout their duration. Yet, just like a dream, now that they
were winding down, the Games seemed to have come and gone

in no time. I was heartsick over leaving the Olympics and all my
new friends—one friend in particular.

"Shawn, want to get together with everyone tonight?" Taylor had
asked me over the phone earlier that day. "It'll be fun!"

I didn't even need my agent's help this time. My parents thought
Taylor was great, and they immediately gave their permission. After
all, you're only in China for the Olympics once, right? A group of us
Olympic athletes went out together, laughed, had "flip contests," and
walked through the city to the Olympic Village.

As I walked down the street, I felt so alive. I enjoyed being with
people who totally understood what the past few weeks had been
like. I figured it would be hard to describe to friends who hadn't
been here.

We ate, reminisced, and said our good-byes at about one o'clock
in the morning.

"I'm going to miss you guys," I said, giving the last friend a big
hug, my e-mail address, and my phone number so we could stay in
touch. Eventually, everyone went back to their rooms.

Everyone except Taylor.

"Want to sit down?" he asked. We were in the lobby of my
hotel, but he led me up to the hospitality room on the first floor
where we could sit and talk. I was so thankful to finally have some
time alone with him. Our late-night balcony-to-balcony chats were
sometimes the only thing that had kept me going. Though I was
sad that he had a girlfriend back home, I respected that he was not
a cheater.

And so we talked. And talked. We covered a million topics—
including our hometowns and our lives outside Olympic training.
We moved past the "getting to know you" topics into the deeper
questions of life. I'm not sure why I felt so comfortable with Taylor,
but I did open up to him about things that I'm normally too shy
to share.

He told me things about his life as well. "I broke up with my girlfriend," he blurted out.

I tried to keep my face from breaking into a smile. Instead, I gave him a concerned look and said simply, "I'm sorry for what you must be going through."

Just then, we were interrupted by a hotel staffer who was trying to clean up. "I have to service this area," he said, pointing to the clock. "It's late."

He was right. By this time it was nearly two o'clock in the morning, but there was no way I wanted this night to end! I didn't think staying out longer would be a problem. After all, I'd been living in the Olympic Village without real adult supervision—other than coaches who made sure we didn't pig out at the free food line. I had gotten used to setting my own schedule and figuring out when it was appropriate to arrive and when it was appropriate to go. I'd been forced to grow up a bit and start taking care of my own laundry, money, food, and living areas.

"Do you need to go?" Taylor asked me.

"Let's talk a bit more," I suggested, figuring it was okay. Because I was sharing a room with Sheryl, I didn't think my parents would be worried about where I might be. Plus, they had allowed me to go to the Oakley party, which ended pretty late.

"Okay," he said, taking my hand. "Follow me." Not having anywhere to go, we walked around the hotel until we found an area on the second floor that had a huge sofa stretching along the entire wall below a gigantic window. We made ourselves comfortable and kept talking. My back was to the staircase, and Taylor was facing the stairs. The area was separated from the rest of the room by a curtain, so although it was public, we weren't bothering anyone and no one was bothering us.

That's where we kissed.

What a magically romantic moment! Though we'd known each

other for only a few weeks, we'd gone through an extremely intense experience together. As a result, we had become close friends in a short period of time. We were at the Olympics . . . *at the Olympics* . . . enjoying the last few hours we had in China.

"What are we doing?" he asked me. He was holding my hand.

"What do you mean?"

"I mean, where is this going?" he said. "You and me."

"Well, you live in Colorado, and I live in Iowa," I said.

The kiss created a whole new depth of conversation. Would we try to stay a couple when we went back home? *Were* we even "a couple"? If he went to college, how could we see each other?

Even though it was a tough conversation, I was having the time of my life. I was heady with the romance, intoxicated by his company, and thrilled by the long-awaited kiss.

I remember what happened next very vividly.

Because Taylor was facing the stairs, he saw them coming first. A look of absolute panic crossed his face. My mom and dad were marching down the staircase, looking disheveled and furious.

"What do you think you are doing?" they asked us. "Do you even know what time it is?"

I completely lost my ability to speak. I'd never been more humiliated in my life. There I was, planning out my romantic future with Taylor, only to have my mommy and daddy come downstairs to tell me I'd missed curfew. If I could have disappeared, I would have. Taylor jumped to his feet and apologized.

I figured my dad would kill him, but he simply said, "Let me call you a cab."

We said a hasty good-bye, my face hot with embarrassment and anger. Dad walked Taylor out the door and hailed a taxi.

"What were you doing?" my mom asked me as we walked back upstairs. "You are only *sixteen*."

"I've been living without you for a month!"

"You scared us silly! We're in a foreign country, and all of a sudden we realize we have no idea where you are in the middle of the night!"

The most romantic night of my life had ended with me feeling like a sixth grader.

To this day, my parents and I disagree about the propriety of my decision to stay up with Taylor on our last night in Beijing. Of course, we all know that breaking away is a normal part of growing up and that we won't always agree on what's best.

About six months later, though, my mom and I would learn what it's like to deal with teenage separation issues on a very public stage.

Lesson I've Learned

All the way through the Olympics, I saw everyone around me as a competitor, so I closed myself off from letting anyone in. It took me a while to trust that people outside my family were not approaching me with an ulterior motive. Since then I've realized the importance of balancing caution with making yourself vulnerable. You need relationships as part of your life.

CHAPTER 19

PROUD TO BE AN AMERICAN

The ache for home lives in all of us.
—*Maya Angelou*

By August 24, the evening of the closing ceremonies, I was ready for my Olympic experience to come to an end. America had dominated, winning a total of 110 medals. That included thirty-six gold, thirty-eight silver, and thirty-six bronze. Four of those medals, I could barely believe, were mine.

The ceremonies were being held in the National Stadium, also known as the Bird's Nest because its exposed beams form a latticework pattern, making the building look like a gigantic nest. I joined other athletes at the Olympic Village, and we boarded buses that took us to the stadium. Once there, we gathered in an underground tunnel, where we prepared to walk into the closing ceremonies. My friend Steven Lopez pulled me up onto his shoulders so I could get a better view of my surroundings.

As we were about to enter the stadium, I saw Taylor with some other US athletes. I dropped from Steven's shoulders, thanked him for the lift, and began talking with Taylor.

"Sorry about last night," I said to him, though he waved it off.

"I have parents too," he said, laughing. "Who are you walking with?" Usually, athletes walk into the arena with their teams, but my team members had returned home, back to their normal lives. I was so exhausted by this point that "normal life" was beginning to look better and better.

"Would you believe I don't have a team anymore?"

"Sure you do," he said, putting his arm around my shoulder. (Despite his nickname "Mini Phinney," Taylor is six-feet-five-inches tall, so I'm sure we made quite the pair.) "The cycling team can adopt you."

The closing ceremonies were amazing. Walking into the stadium as a member of the United States Olympic Team was one of the proudest moments of my life. From all corners of the stadium, athletes from the competing nations marched in under their flags. The Chinese delegation got a huge roar from the hometown crowd, which made me happy. Something about being there with Chow made me feel so much affection for the host country's athletes.

Many of the athletes took out their phones and video cameras and recorded themselves when they appeared on the giant screen. I tried to soak it all in—the fireworks, the singing, the dancing. In many ways, the Beijing Olympics were the most successful in Olympic history—a whopping thirty-nine world records were broken—and the elaborate but lighthearted closing ceremonies were a fitting way to end a wonderful competition.

Soon after, I was heading to the airport with my parents and Sheryl. "I hear people are gathering at the airport at home," Mom told us. I smiled at the thought of friends meeting me at Des Moines International Airport for the kind of warm celebration that can be spontaneously generated only in small towns. The thought of home—my own bed and my dog, Tucker—was so tantalizing, I could barely stand it.

Then Sheryl's phone rang. I had been invited to appear on the *Late Show with David Letterman.*

"Why would they ask me?" I wondered.

"Shawn, people back home love you. Some are calling you America's sweetheart."

After figuring out the time differences and doing a bit of rescheduling, we decided we could probably make it to New York before the show.

We left Beijing at 10:30 a.m., were in the air for twelve hours, and landed in Chicago at 10:15 a.m. on the same day we left. That blew my mind and wreaked havoc on my body's internal clock. But there was no time for jet lag.

Once we landed in Chicago, Sheryl and I would head immediately to another gate for a flight to New York, while Mom and Dad would fly home to Des Moines. We had one hour before our flight took off, which sounded like plenty of time.

As soon as we got off the plane, Sheryl said, "Okay, let's say our good-byes, because we have to go through customs, baggage claim, rebooking, and other sorts of hoops associated with international travel." I hugged Mom and Dad and started running through the airport, towing a little suitcase. We thought we'd made it until we emerged from all of the rebooking and looked up at the terminal signs.

"Oh no," Sheryl said, looking at our tickets. "Our plane's at the very end of a totally different terminal!"

We were completely deflated, but fortunately Sheryl was used to solving problems.

She explained the situation to a security guard, who nodded and said, "Follow me."

The last time we'd obeyed that command, we ended up in a strange Chinese purse warehouse. But knowing we had little choice,

Sheryl and I followed him into the lower level of the airport where baggage is kept.

A van was waiting for us, and we jumped in just before it sped off. I mean, it flew through the bowels of the airport and out onto the tarmac. I felt like I was in some sort of action movie. We were dodging airplanes and crossing runways until the driver pulled up right next to our plane. We walked straight onto the plane and settled into our seats. If our flight took off immediately, as it was scheduled to do, we'd be able to get to the set just in time for the taping.

"I can't believe we made it," I said to Sheryl. "Those guards were amazing!" I buckled my seat belt and exhaled in relief. Finally, I'd reached the end of all the drama.

Suddenly, the pilot got on the intercom and made a very strange announcement.

"Ladies and gentlemen," he began, "I'm sorry, but our flight is going to be delayed while we wait for another copilot." He explained that the scheduled copilot had been injured and needed medical treatment.

I looked at Sheryl and couldn't help but laugh. We had done everything we could to get to New York on time. Perhaps it simply wasn't meant to be. My interview was scheduled for only about three minutes. I wasn't sure the effort was worth it.

"Everything happens for a reason," I said as we sat on the tarmac. However, I had no idea that the reason was me!

A few minutes later, the pilot came back to our seats and gave us the real story. Apparently the original copilot was a big fan of mine. When he heard he would be flying me to New York, he was so excited he actually jumped up and hit his head, hard.

I felt bad for the guy. Despite the delay, we made it to the Letterman studio in time. After so many hours of traveling, I looked terrible. Yet when our black Escalade SUV pulled up to the studio, a line of paparazzi was waiting for me.

"Wow!" I said once we made it inside. "I feel like a rock star!"

I knew I'd been getting a lot of attention in Beijing. But in New York? The Olympics were over, after all.

Thankfully, the hair and makeup artists were miracle workers, and after putting on a cute black dress, I felt ready for the cameras.

Backstage, I got to meet actor and comedian Tracy Morgan. "I hope my six-year-old daughter grows up to be the next Shawn Johnson," he said. He hugged me, and I felt so touched by all the warmth that people—both celebrities and everyday folks—had been showing me.

By the time I walked out onto the stage—to the tune "Fields of Gold," no less—I felt like a million bucks. David Letterman was so funny and kind. (He did joke that cameras in Beijing had caught the Chinese gymnasts sucking on pacifiers between routines, which made everyone laugh.) He made me feel so comfortable that I wasn't intimidated at all about being on his show. After being on Chinese TV, where I couldn't understand one word of my interviewer's questions, David Letterman was a piece of cake.

The interview went well—except that the studio's temperature is kept at 54 degrees! I was freezing in my little black dress. Letterman must have enjoyed my interview time, too, because my three-minute segment stretched into a piece that ran over ten minutes. All the effort to get to the show was totally worth it.

Once again, I was ready to go home. Family friend Donna Tweeten of Hy-Vee had flown to New York to help me get back to Iowa. Sheryl lived in New York, so she planned to head home after we grabbed a bite to eat. I changed into something more comfortable for travel and headed out to a waiting car—only to find an enormous number of fans and media waiting outside for me. I shook hands, posed for photos, and signed autographs until I really had to leave. Some poor guy chased our car all the way down the street. After a few stoplights, he caught up to us, so I rolled down the window and signed a piece of paper for him.

It was a little thrilling and a little disconcerting. I was surprised that even jaded New Yorkers seemed to notice me in the Manhattan restaurant where we stopped to eat.

Donna just laughed. "You better get used to it," she said.

When we finally arrived in Des Moines at 2 a.m., there was no welcome party to cheer me off the plane, just a couple of reporters and a camera crew. Apparently four thousand people had gathered earlier to meet me, but they left when they heard I'd gone to New York. I was thankful for the chance to simply go back to my house, my parents, Tucker, and our cats, Max and Vern.

When we reached my neighborhood, I saw balloons tied on all my neighbors' mailboxes and signs dotting the streets welcoming me home. Someone had even decorated my driveway with chalk.

Finally, I thought. *A normal life.*

I had no idea how much my hometown had supported me until the next evening, when a white limousine showed up at my house and drove me to the Wells Fargo Arena. Three police officers (two in uniform and one undercover) met me there, along with Chow and Li. We waited around in the greenroom, wondering who would possibly take time out of their day to see us.

Imagine my surprise when I walked out on stage and saw over *six thousand* cheering fans! My parents, along with Coach Chow and Coach Li, were already on the stage. In the front row, my cousin Tori was crying her eyes out.

The Valley High School choir was there, along with all of Chow's gymnasts. I got to see just about every teacher I've ever had, as well as an awesome band called The Nadas, who wrote and performed a song just for me. The city proclaimed that September would be Shawn Johnson Month. I also got to shoot about twenty T-shirts out of a T-shirt cannon into the crowd, which was more fun than it should have been.

The audience was going crazy, in particular one teenage guy who'd made a sign that read, "Marry Me, Shawn?" I looked at him and smiled at the joke. But when I saw his eyes, I realized it was no joke. He seemed to be serious.

This homecoming was one of the best moments of my life. It's one thing to be recognized on the streets of New York or Beijing. It's quite another to come back and realize that your hometown has been behind you the entire way. Thank you, West Des Moines.

I wasn't able to stay home for long. After just two days, I headed to the Democratic National Convention.

At the height of Mary Lou Retton's popularity, she was a supporter of Ronald Reagan and appeared in a variety of televised ads supporting him. Later she delivered the Pledge of Allegiance with 1996 Olympic medalist Kerri Strug at the 2004 Republican National Convention.

I, however, was not eager to come out of the Olympics and into the political arena. I'm not into politics *at all*. Even though there was a huge presidential contest going on in 2008, it's hard to perfect your backflip with a full twist on the beam while keeping up with the debates. But in spite of that, people started trying to discern my innermost thoughts on the government.

Their main evidence?

A T-shirt.

Yes, I'd shown up at an event wearing a shirt that had a peace symbol on it, and people started saying I was making an antiwar statement. Also, on one of my interviews with Bob Costas I wore peace earrings, which set the Internet abuzz. Was I trying to secretly endorse Obama? Was I opposing the troops? Did I think it was time to pull out of Iraq?

Well, it's not an interesting story. I just bought the T-shirt because I liked the way it looked. (I got it at my local Target, where there were racks of these tees.) Plus, at the Olympics, the peace sign was everywhere. Since we had to overcome so many language barriers with other athletes, we gestured to communicate. Perhaps in the 1960s, putting two fingers up was some sort of countercultural political statement. But at the Olympic Village in 2008, it was simply a way to say good-bye, an acknowledgment that we were leaving each other with good wishes. Instead of "peace," we'd say "peace out," or "deuces" (because we held up two fingers).

Having said that, I was honored to be invited to the Democratic National Convention to lead the Pledge of Allegiance. I didn't look at it as a chance to come out and support a candidate for the White House. Rather, I saw it as a patriotic privilege, a way to be a part of history. Barack Obama was being officially selected as the Democratic nominee for president, and I would get to be there.

The convention was held in Denver, right after the Olympics concluded. Once backstage, I met Vice President Al Gore, Stevie Wonder, will.i.am, Sheryl Crow, and many other people.

Then it was my turn to take the stage. Of course, leading the Pledge of Allegiance is a little different than performing on the beam. What if I froze? What if I forgot the words? Thankfully, they provided a teleprompter for me, which took away my anxiety a bit. I walked out on the stage on that perfectly sunny day and led the crowd in our pledge. I was so proud to be an Olympian, and even prouder to be an American.

"One nation under God, indivisible, with liberty and justice for all," I finished.

The crowd roared.

Lesson I've Learned

Don't ever forget where you came from. Appreciate the people who've helped make you who you are.

CHAPTER 20

THE BEST OF BOTH WORLDS

Happiness is a journey, not a destination.
—*Alfred Souza*

"You looked great on Letterman. We miss you!"

In the weeks following the Olympics, I received texts like these from my high school friends, many of whom hadn't seen me since the previous school year. Even after I was back in the States, I had a number of commitments to keep, so I was busy jetting from one place to another. I looked forward to hanging out with my friends again, but for a while their only chances to see me were my TV appearances with Letterman, Oprah, Ellen DeGeneres, and Leno.

Though I didn't feel close to many girls during elementary school, I'd developed a core group of friends in high school. The nine of us had grown up together in West Des Moines, and I appreciated how supportive they were. I've always been quieter than everyone else, probably because of my focus on gymnastics. But my friends didn't mind.

They didn't treat me like I was "Shawn Johnson, the Olympian."

They'd known me since I was teased on the playground because "Shawn Johnson" was a boy's name. So they understood where I'd come from and appreciated where I'd ended up. They were so much fun, and when I was with them, they gave me a sense of freedom I never had when I was training.

While I always loved hearing from my friends, I also began receiving texts from kids who never would have considered me their friend before: "When are you coming back? We can't wait to see you again." Suddenly, I'd become very popular!

As much as I wanted to get back into the routine of high school, it would have to wait. The 2008 US men's and women's gymnastics teams, along with former Olympic medalists like Shannon Miller, reunited in early September in Reno, Nevada. We were there to kick off the Tour of Gymnastics Superstars, which sounded so cool . . . like we were some sort of rock band traveling to appease our rabid fan base!

The two-month trek across the nation gave us a chance to see the Americans who'd been rooting for us to bring home the gold from Beijing. After spending so much time explaining what it was like to be an Olympic athlete, I was thrilled to be with the only group of people who truly understood that experience.

My parents were a little less enthusiastic. I think they had been looking forward to me staying home. We had all just lived through the most intense year of our lives—one that kept us busy and too often separated from one another. Between long hours of training in the gym, making travel arrangements, and taping endorsements, we'd experienced lots of stress and hardly any time together.

When they discovered that Tori could accompany me, however, they felt better about letting me go. Once all the performers arrived in Reno, we immediately began learning and rehearsing an entirely new production before going on a thirty-seven-city bus tour across America. We weren't burdened by the pressure and competitiveness of the Olympics, so we got to have more fun. On my floor routine, for example, I ran out with my arms raised, and two people slipped silks around my arms. Then, like Peter Pan, I was lifted up off the ground to do aerial tricks. It was exhilarating!

We traveled all over the country. Our stop in San Diego included a *Frosted Pink with a Twist* TV special. I'd done charity work for years with this organization, which focuses on educating people about cancers that primarily affect women. We performed as they taped a live show, hosted by Olympians Shannon Miller and Scott Hamilton. But the show included more than gymnastics; amazing singers like Natasha Bedingfield, Jesse McCartney, Kenny Loggins, and Carole King entertained through their music in one big, star-studded event. Working on *Frosted Pink with a Twist* was especially rewarding because my paternal grandmother is a cancer survivor.

For the entire tour, different musical guests appeared on stage with us, including actor Mitchel Musso, who played Oliver in the TV series *Hannah Montana*. I enjoyed getting to know him because my life always felt a little divided, like Miley's on *Hannah Montana*. I felt like there was a glamorous Shawn on TV and in print ads, but the real Shawn was just a regular girl from West Des Moines.

The tour was fun, but it wasn't as glitzy as one might think. We lived like gypsies on a gigantic tour bus without a shower. We performed several nights a week. Afterward, we'd run through the drive-through at McDonald's. For the first time in recent memory, I was able to eat whatever I wanted, which felt decadent and liberating.

After we ate, we'd laugh and joke around on the bus, eventually falling asleep as mile after mile of America passed by on the other side of the windows. Around four o'clock in the morning, we'd roll into a new city. We'd have to wake up, get our luggage from underneath the bus, check into a hotel, and sleep there until around ten o'clock. Then we'd start all over again—one show after another, seeing the entire country one town at a time. We even performed in Des Moines at the Wells Fargo Arena.

Tori and I were together nonstop for three months. We saw each other at our best and our worst, and we probably fought more than we ever had before. Having said that, Tori has always been like a sister to me, and I was so grateful that she came with me.

Tori's nineteenth birthday fell during our tour, and I wanted to surprise her. Even though we were in a strange city, I was able to arrange to have a decorated cake delivered to our hotel. I gathered everyone into our room while Tori was in another part of the building. Then I called her, asking her to come back to the room right away because someone had gotten hurt. She rushed in, only to find me holding a large, candle-topped cake as our friends sang "Happy Birthday."

Another highlight of the tour came the evening that the Make-a-Wish Foundation connected me with Sidney, a little girl battling leukemia who had asked to meet me. Like me, she was a gymnast. When the tour came to her city, not only did I spend time with her and her family before our performance, I also arranged for Sidney to do her own floor routine during halftime. A live band provided the music, and the crowd gave her an enthusiastic response. I'll never forget that night, and I hope she won't either.

The tour wrapped up right before Thanksgiving. After Tori and I said good-bye to our new friends, we went back home for the holidays. It had been one of the most purely fun times of my life, but I looked forward to getting home and living a more quiet and less dramatic life. I planned on enjoying Thanksgiving and Christmas with my parents and my pets. Then in January, I would go back to Valley to complete my high school career.

That was the plan, anyway . . . and then *Dancing with the Stars* called.

PART 3

Dancing through Life

Walking out . . . minutes left.
My heart is racing. . . .
His eyes locked on mine
with a sense of serenity.
Our fingers intertwine.
Butterflies flutter.
Stars race around.
With a loud applause
we take our ground.
Cameras, lights,
breath held high.
He pulls me close;
I close my eyes.
One last moment
with so much to say . . .
Thank you.
I'm sorry.
Will it all be okay?
You just need to let go.
Dance to the moon.
Feel the clouds.
Sing a tune.

Take a risk.
Make that leap
you'll never regret but
want to keep.
Every new second
you grow inside:
healing, repairing,
fears aside.
I thank you for everything
you've given to me,
things to cherish
for eternity.
You spin me out,
hand in hand.
Smiling at me,
you understand.
All I can hope
is I've made you proud.
With the melody going,
we dance to a crowd.

CHAPTER 21

HOLLYWOOD, HERE I COME!

Dance as though no one is watching you.
Love as though you have never been hurt before.
Sing as though no one can hear you.
Live as though heaven is on earth.

—*Alfred Souza*

LATE ONE AFTERNOON shortly after I'd returned home from tour,
I was driving through West Des Moines. *This looks different,*
I thought. Then it dawned on me: I'd never seen my town at 4 p.m.
on a weekday.

I was beginning to experience life as I'd never experienced
it before. Did I want to spend the afternoon shopping? I could,
because I wasn't busy on the bars in the gym. Did I need to run to
the store at midnight? No problem, because I no longer had to get
up early to train. Did I want to eat that burger? Definitely, because
I didn't have to keep such a tight rein on my weight.

I could get used to this new sense of freedom!

After a couple of weeks untethered to the gym or a coach, I realized how much I loved normal life. Yet I realized that my schedule
could soon change once again. That's because I was waiting to see
if I would be formally invited to appear on *Dancing with the Stars*.

While I was still on tour, Sheryl had called to talk with me about that possibility. When I first heard that the producers might be interested in me, I thought, *A completely new challenge? A chance to push my body in a whole new way?* I was always up for that. There was just one little problem.

"*Dancing with the Stars*?" I said into my phone. "But I can't dance."

"You don't have to know before you're a contestant. That's the whole point," my agent assured me. "In fact, the producers have invited you to go out to Los Angeles to see the show that's currently taping. You can see how this season works. If it seems fun, you can be on season eight in a couple of months."

"You know this will mean that you won't be able to go back to school in January," Mom reminded me. My mom and dad had tried so hard to keep my life in the category of "normal." We'd always said that I'd never miss the high school experience, no matter what. The Olympics were an obvious exception. Now that the Games were over, it was time to return to school—to backpacks, homework, football games, and pep rallies. But as much as I loved Valley High, this was an amazing opportunity.

"Well, we can at least go out there and see what it's like," I said to my mom. "If you don't like the look of it, I don't have to do it."

So during a break in the tour in early November, Sheryl and I visited the set of *Dancing with the Stars*, season seven. We got to watch the taping of the show, meet the producers, and see all of the behind-the-scenes action. It was dazzling! All of the beautiful costumes, the cameras, the elegant dances . . . it was like a fairy tale.

"What do you think? Do you want to come?" one of the producers asked me after the show.

"I'd love to do it," I said.

Despite interest on both our parts, some details still needed to be worked out. Specifically, because I was seventeen, a minor and the youngest person ever to be considered for a spot on the show, my *DWTS* contract had to be reviewed by a Los Angeles County judge.

I was sitting in Chicago's O'Hare Airport about a month later, waiting for a flight back to Des Moines, when my phone rang. It was Sheryl.

"So . . . I guess you'd better buy some dancing shoes!" she said. She told me *DWTS* had just extended an invitation for me to appear on the show after the judge had approved my contract. The one condition: a chaperone would have to accompany me to every rehearsal.

My mom agreed to come with me to Hollywood and serve as my chaperone. Her boss suggested she take a leave of absence, but my mom, not wanting to take advantage of her company, left her job. By February, we were in Los Angeles preparing for the upcoming season.

Dancing with the Stars pairs professional dancers with celebrity cast members. Many of the dancers return season after season, while the celebrities rotate in and out. This is what keeps the show fresh and exciting. During season eight, the celebrities included professional athletes, reality TV stars, musicians, and actors. During the first few days, we got to know one another. Many members of the cast told me they'd seen me in the Olympics, and I knew many of them through their work as well. Almost all of us expressed concern about our ability to dance and perform in front of America. Even though we came from very different backgrounds, we got along well right from the start.

I got to be great friends with some of the other contestants, like Lil' Kim and Steve-O. My absolute favorite was Chuck Wicks, a country singer who was competing along with his girlfriend, Julianne Hough. While she was a professional dancer, actress, and *DWTS* alum, Chuck was just a regular guy who grew up on a farm. I identified with him because he was a down-to-earth person like me amid all the glamour and sparkle of Hollywood.

Each of the "celebrities" (though I've never considered myself one) was assigned a professional dancer based on various factors, including height, age, and personality. Mark Ballas was my partner, and I was so thankful for the pairing. He is an accomplished ball-room dancer and musician who had won season six of *DWTS* with Olympic figure skater Kristi Yamaguchi.

Once we were paired up, Mark showed amazing patience in spite of how little I knew. I was the type of girl who stood against the wall during high school dances because I didn't want my class-mates to see me dancing. Mark explained the moves to me in the most competent and professional manner.

Having said that, he was also very playful and silly—which made backstage life at *DWTS* unpredictable. He was twenty-two years old and I was seventeen, but he sometimes acted like he was the younger one. In the weeks leading up to the show, I began to see this more clearly. For example, once I walked into the studio and found him asleep on the floor.

"Um . . . what are you doing?" I asked. I was used to starting practice early and ending late.

He barely even acknowledged me. "I have to take a nap, babe."

"I just got here!" I protested. "What's your problem?"

He didn't move.

"Let's work!" I said, realizing that I really needed the practice. The first week's dance was the waltz, a moderately fast dance in which we had to elegantly glide in circles, taking one step for each beat. Every move was carefully choreographed, so I needed to get into the studio.

Who am I kidding? I'm always serious about practice. While the other contestants complained about the hours of rehearsal each day, it was a vacation compared to Olympic-level training, when I had to put in hours of work *before* lunch and then return to the gym and do it all again *after* lunch.

I nudged Mark with my foot to see if he'd wake up, but it was no use. He was determined to take that nap!

Still, I was in good hands. He taught me everything I needed to know about each dance, pushing me further than I thought I could go. He also had a great way of calming me down. Sometimes, he'd just softly encourage me. Other times, he'd get out his guitar and play me a song. I was thankful to have a partner like Mark. I knew I'd have fun, even if I didn't bring home the mirror ball trophy.

And by the way, the first time I saw the mirror ball, I couldn't believe it. The highly coveted prize is something anyone could make for five dollars with a glue gun, a Styrofoam ball, tiny mirrored tiles, and a little ingenuity. Nevertheless, I wanted it more than anything.

Every week, Mark and I competed against other couples by dancing for three judges: Len Goodman, Bruno Tonioli, and Carrie Ann Inaba. After watching us dance, they each scored us on a ten-point scale. In addition, the at-home viewing audience would vote. As long as we didn't receive the lowest combined total of judges' points and audience votes, we'd get to stay on the show for another week.

We practiced hard to prepare for the first day of the show, but I was absolutely terrified when that day finally arrived.

Even though I'd competed on a worldwide stage, with cameras following my every move, I never felt more anxious than that morning when I woke up and headed to the ABC studio around ten o'clock. My assistant, Tracey—yes, I had an assistant—greeted Mark and me and then ushered us into all of the preshow preparations. Tracey called me Peanut, a term of endearment that I loved.

First, she took us to our trailers. Mine was Trailer 22, and Mark's was 17. We joked that we should switch so our trailer numbers would match our ages. I couldn't believe I had a trailer, and I wondered what celebrities had used it over the years. Mine had a couch, a bathroom, a vanity, and a microwave. Plus, it was full of beautiful flowers that people had sent to me . . . including one lovely bunch from Mitchel Musso, my new friend from the Tour of Gymnastics Superstars. Mitchel even stopped by the studio one day to wish me luck.

After Tracey showed me my trailer, Mark and I did a quick run-through onstage. This is how the cameramen determine where the cameras should be during the dance and how the viewing audience will see every important foot move. They know exactly what's coming before the show goes live.

Next, I was taken to get my hair and makeup done. In gymnastics, we weren't supposed to wear heavy makeup, except to accentuate our eyes. Hairstyling before a meet usually meant pulling our hair back in a tight ponytail. So getting the full treatment for *DWTS* was absolutely amazing. My hairstylist was so talented at creating the perfect look for me—elegant and simple. She created a loose, wavy style by pulling some of my hair back with diamond flower pins. I felt like a princess.

Hair and makeup took about three hours, and during most of the time I was sitting in the chair, I could hear Mark playing his guitar. *Girls have to go through so much more than guys do,* I thought.

By the time the show was about to go live, I was shaking. A crew member went out onstage first to prepare the audience. Then came the music. Flashing lights meant we were about to be officially announced to the viewers. That first night, we were supposed to walk down some stairs and onto the stage as our names were announced.

I almost couldn't bear it. Just after they introduced the couple in front of us, we were given the signal to start. Then, as I walked down the stairs—looking like a princess and holding Mark's hand—I almost tripped in my three-inch heels. Since I wasn't comfortable in them, I simply misjudged the steps and lost my balance. Thankfully, it was *almost* unnoticeable. Mark was right there to straighten me, and the cameras had almost moved off us by the time I slipped. But still, I'd almost blown it during the first few seconds of the show, and that put me even more on edge.

As we waited backstage while the other contestants competed, I became more and more anxious. "Can we go over it one more time?" I asked Mark as we waited to compete. "I've totally forgotten it!"

Mark laughed at me and assured me that everything would work out. Right before we were announced, we did our promo, which is the little segment where we smile and laugh backstage while the camera pans over us.

Then it was time to dance. We walked hand in hand out onto the stage. Once we got into position, Mark whispered to me, "Just stay calm. It's just the two of us . . . no one else."

While that was *technically* true—we were the only two *onstage*—we were about to dance in front of a live studio audience, on live national TV, for an audience of millions watching from home.

Still, his words somehow calmed me. I closed my eyes and took a deep breath. Mark put his face against mine as we waited for our cue.

I heard the show's host, Tom Bergeron, announce, "Dancing the waltz . . . Shawn Johnson and her partner, Mark Ballas!"

The music started, and we took off. The dance was elegant and enchanting, and I seemed to hit every mark. As we danced, I felt like I had no worries in the world, and I simply enjoyed the moment. When we finished the waltz, I was grinning from ear to ear. I'd done it.

Rather, *we'd* done it, and I'd had the time of my life.

I could tell Mark was proud of me, as were the judges. Carrie Ann was so emotional that her eyes filled with tears. She told me, "You have the power to move people with your dancing."

I thought, *Okay, if the whole show is like this, I've got it.*

Of course, I'd soon learn that every week would not be as easy.

Lesson I've Learned

Stepping out of your comfort zone may be scary at first. But it's worth the risk to see how far you can go.

CHAPTER 22

FINDING MY SPACE

Courage doesn't always roar. Sometimes courage is the quiet
voice at the end of the day saying, "I will try again tomorrow."
—*Mary Anne Radmacher*

WHEN THE JUDGE signed off on my participation in *Dancing
with the Stars* by ordering that I have a chaperone with me every
second, he put my mom and me in an extremely awkward position. As much as I love my mom, I found it difficult to be with her
every moment. After all, while I was in China for five weeks, I had
to do my own laundry and get my own meals. Then, when I went
on tour with my Olympic friends, I was on my own for another
two and a half months. Now, suddenly I couldn't leave my mom's
presence. I enjoyed hanging out with Mark and learning new dance
moves, and I would have preferred a little space. Mark never really
understood why my mom had to be there, and I know she sensed
his annoyance.

"Mom," I said to her one day in frustration, "I'm old enough to
take care of myself."

"Don't you think I know that?" she responded, fighting back tears.

Of course, she was in a terrible bind. She couldn't disobey the judge's orders, but she didn't want to hang out on the set with me when she wasn't wanted. On top of that, she was apart from my dad for the first time in thirty years. Though he came out for the show's tapings, he had to spend most of each week at home tending his business.

My mom did everything she could to make things work. She read stacks of novels while sitting in the back of the studio where we rehearsed. She learned to navigate the terrible traffic in LA so she could get us wherever we needed to go. Each morning, she'd run to a little shop called the Coffee Bean to get me coffee while I did early-morning phone interviews in my pajamas.

My mom's presence may have made me feel smothered at times, but it didn't help that I was labeled on the show as the naive teenager. Maybe it's just the nature of reality TV, but there seemed to be a narrative for every cast member. And each of us needed to conform to our role in the story. I was usually depicted as inexperienced and wide-eyed. When dispensing advice, the judges kept mentioning that my dances were "age appropriate." My true self didn't really match the girl they were portraying me to be. Maybe they mistook my natural shyness for excessive sheltering.

One day later in the season, I went into the studio and discovered that the producers had staged a prom, complete with a disco ball and cheesy costumes, for Mark and me. Yes, I was only seventeen, but the "She's so young" theme got to be a little much. At times I wanted to say, "Okay, guys, I'm not eight."

Despite my discomfort at how I was sometimes portrayed, my high-scoring waltz did a lot to alleviate my nerves. On week two, however, Mark and I were assigned the salsa—a dance that includes *a lot* of hip movement.

"Sorry, but my hips have never moved that way," I told a frustrated Mark. He'd been patiently showing me exactly what I was supposed to do. He tried different approaches. He cajoled. He begged. He ordered. He joked. He even unashamedly performed the female role to help me visualize what I should do.

I just shook my head. "In gymnastics, we simply *don't* move like that. We aren't allowed to."

The more he told me to relax, the more locked up I got. I wasn't sure if I wanted to scream or cry. But instead of having a complete meltdown in the studio, I ran to the bathroom, locking the door before bawling my eyes out.

"Shawn," I heard my mom yell from the other side of the door. "Please come out."

Mark was completely stunned. At least that's what his tone of voice suggested. "Seriously?" I heard him ask my mom.

There was no way I was coming out. Tears streamed down my face, and I grabbed some toilet paper to blow my nose.

"I want to go home!" I cried. "I don't like this. I don't want to do it. I'm done."

"That's fine!" my mom said through the door. "Come on out. You don't have to do it."

About forty-five minutes later, I finally unlocked the door and emerged with swollen, puffy eyes. Mark, tired of waiting for me, was gone by the time I came out. I was quiet on the drive back to our apartment.

"I've never been able to get out there and perform for anyone," Mom said gently. "I'm not even able to dance with your dad in public. I don't want you to be like me. I want you to experience things."

Once we got to our apartment, I went to my room and tried to talk myself into doing the salsa.

Okay. You just have to try, I thought.

Though I was mortified, I went back to the studio the next day and gave it my all. We were behind. Because of my bathroom incident, we'd missed a whole day of practice.

When it came time to perform, I thought I *might* be able to make it past elimination. I had at least three things going for me. First, I had an amazing outfit. Though I looked a little like the Chiquita banana girl, the costume made me feel glamorous. Second, the hairstylists once again did something unique with my hair, which may have looked a bit strange in person, but came off well on TV. And last, I had Mark, who was encouraging me the entire way.

"Dancing the salsa," Tom announced, "Shawn Johnson and her partner, Mark Ballas!" I took a deep breath.

When the music started, I felt completely ready to go. All my inhibitions melted away, and I danced with all my heart. I could tell the crowd was very supportive, and once again, I had a blast.

"You are the cutest thing," Bruno said after Mark and I finished, completely out of breath. "But I want you to be more naughty and more flirtatious."

"She's only seventeen," Tom responded.

Though the judges weren't as lavish with their praise as they had been the first week, I think their responses showed what a strange position I'd been put in. I was in the space between "already" and "not yet"—past childhood but not quite an adult. Could the young, naive girl dance a salsa? Somehow I'd pulled it off and managed to make the cut.

After that very challenging performance, I began thinking about gymnastics and its place in my life. One night, I went on YouTube and watched some of my Olympic performances. I felt something stirring in my heart. Was I really done with the sport that had been such a part of me for so long? As I sat in front of my computer, I struggled with my future. Those videos brought to mind so many questions . . . questions I honestly couldn't answer.

Was it even possible to go back?

Had I been out of practice for too long?

What would my motivation be in going back?

Was I willing to do it all again?

If I went back to training, would I lose all of my opportunities in other areas?

Could I come back as good as I'd been before? Or maybe even better?

Would I move out of my parents' house, and if so, where would I train?

Would it be worth it?

I realized how much my feelings about gymnastics were shifting back and forth. Before my second week on *Dancing with the Stars*, I easily would have said "no way!" to the idea of going back to the gym.

But the following week, as Mark and I were preparing to perform the fox-trot, I was seriously leaning toward going back. One night, as I wrote in my journal before bed, I ended my entry with a single word:

"Help!"

Lesson I've Learned

When you're in close quarters with family members or friends, give both yourself and them grace. During *Dancing with the Stars*, my mom and I were together almost all the time, so naturally we began to get on each other's nerves. She also happened to be the one person I felt safe letting out my frustration on. I might have been more patient and kind if I'd understood how much pressure she was under. She wasn't used to all the publicity and producers trying to call many of the shots. In a way, she had to watch me grow up under the hands of someone else. Looking back, I'm extremely appreciative of all she did for me during *DWTS*.

CHAPTER 23

AN ARRESTING DEVELOPMENT

The Lord is faithful; he will strengthen you and guard you from the evil one.
—2 Thessalonians 3:3

SOMETHING CHANGED in me after successfully completing that salsa. I felt more confident, more alive . . . almost like I could do anything after making it through that dance. Plus, our fans were very encouraging, and I loved the nickname they'd given us: "Team Shark," a combination of Shawn and Mark.

The third week we were assigned the fox-trot, another elegant, calm, and cool dance. After a good week of practice, I figured we'd either hit it or miss it. But I should have had more confidence because we absolutely nailed it. Not only did we score our first 9, we got our first set of *three* 9s! After giving post-dance interviews, Mark and I were elated as we received high fives from our friends backstage.

As we celebrated, I noticed something odd. For one thing, my parents were nowhere to be seen. They'd been cheering for me as always in the audience, but they weren't there to greet me backstage as they had been after every other performance. My agent was scurrying around more than usual too.

When Sheryl finally slowed down enough for me to walk up to her, she looked as serious as I'd ever seen her.

"What's wrong?" I asked. "Did you see the dance? We nailed it!"

"The dance was great," she said with a brief smile. Then her solemn expression returned.

"Everything okay?"

"We'll talk later," she said.

For the rest of the show, I was anxious. I didn't even watch the other contestants perform. Once the show had ended and we'd done our interviews, Tracey and I walked back to my trailer.

When I opened the door, I was surprised to see that it was full of people—my parents, Sheryl, people from the show, and a huge African American man I'd never seen before. Everyone looked worried, which freaked me out even more.

"What's going on?" I asked.

Slowly they explained the situation. "A man drove from Florida either to kidnap you or to kill you . . . it's impossible to know which," I was told.

My mind was racing. Though they told me all the details they knew, I could barely understand what was happening. Then I heard someone use the word *stalker* for the first time. Shawn Johnson from West Des Moines had a stalker? It just didn't seem real.

But it definitely was. Half a dozen people were in my trailer emphasizing how very real the threat to my life had been. My stalker was a thirty-four-year-old man from Florida. I was horrified to learn that he had made it all the way from his home to the CBS lot in California, where he was apprehended by police officers after jumping the fence.

A security guard told me what they had found in his car: zip ties, duct tape, a knife, a bulletproof vest, a shotgun, and a loaded Colt .45 hidden in a hollowed-out Bible.

The police had also found letters in his vehicle that described his plans to marry me. He'd even hyphenated my last name with his on the papers.

As I was struggling to take all this in, Sheryl spoke. "This is your new bodyguard," she said, motioning to the enormous man beside her. "You need to listen to him and follow his orders."

Suddenly, I had a stalker *and* a bodyguard?

"Shawn, things are going to have to change," the man said very simply. "Do you want to go home?"

"To West Des Moines?" I asked, not really comprehending. "You mean, quit the show?"

My parents looked stricken. We weren't sure what to do.

"Let's go," my mom said. She just wanted to take me home. "Let's get you out of the limelight. It's not worth it."

"Wait a second," my dad said, holding up his hand as if to calm the room. "Shawn is probably better protected here than she would be if we left *Dancing with the Stars* and went back to West Des Moines. . . . What if this guy gets off and comes to find her?"

We discussed our options. We had great law enforcement back home, but we had a bodyguard and security here who were attuned to the situation.

I felt sick to my stomach as I considered my options. I had just gotten comfortable on the show. I was performing the dances well; I was enjoying my new friends; and I finally felt like I had gotten the hang of a new routine. I didn't want to give it all up because of some crazy stranger. After more back-and-forth, I blurted out, "I don't want to quit."

"Okay then," my bodyguard said. "First of all, you're going to have to move to an undisclosed location and check in there under an alias. Don't tell anyone where you're living, not even Mark. The fewer people who know where you are, the better."

I was disappointed. Though the little apartment my mom and I had been assigned in Los Angeles wasn't terribly fancy, it had become "home" to me, much like the Olympic Village had. All the other con-testants—my *DWTS* "family"—were living nearby. I couldn't imag-ine packing up and moving to a strange, new location.

"Second," he continued, "we're going to get you a different car. We don't want to take the chance of anyone recognizing you by what you're driving."

All of these drastic measures made me realize what a big deal this threat was.

"Third, we'll get you a more private location to rehearse," he said. "One without windows so people can't watch you, whether accidentally or intentionally.

"I'm going to be with you at all times. That means that if you go to a store, I'll be there too. If you move from one area of the stage to another, I'll move too." He reminded me that I could still drop out of the competition and head home if I was too rattled by everything. Again, I said I was determined to stay.

When Mark heard that someone had tried to kidnap me, or worse, he got very protective. "Where is he?" Mark said, ready to bust the guy's head. Maksim Chmerkovskiy, another one of the professional dancers, reacted similarly. He puffed out his chest and walked over to me, saying, "I'll take care of you, Shawn. I won't let anybody get you."

Though I appreciated everyone's kindness, I couldn't stop looking over my shoulder, even after we moved into a fantastic hotel that was much nicer than our original apartment. When I was alone in my room, I still felt like someone was watching me. Mom got a restrain-ing order against the stalker to protect me, her, and Mark. This meant that he was ordered to stay one hundred yards away from me and was prohibited from communicating with me or harassing Mom, Dad, or Mark. His bail was set at $35,000.

My bodyguard hadn't been exaggerating when he told me he'd be right with me at all times. "Call me Brother Dave," he said, try-ing to make his presence less intimidating.

I could have just as easily called him Shadow because he followed me everywhere. It took a little getting used to. I remember going to a farmer's market and feeling so odd having a gigantic, muscular man following me as I picked out some asparagus. I soon found out that although Dave *looked* tough, he was actually a big softy. I grew to appreciate the care and competence he showed while watching after me, and we became good friends.

Over the next few days, life was hard. I met with the Los Angeles police department, attorneys, detectives, and bodyguards. All this, while trying to remain competitive on one of America's top reality TV shows. I went to rehearsal and tried to concentrate on my next dance, something called the Lindy Hop. During practice, I was able to force the fear out of my mind long enough to try to figure out my dance moves.

One day in the studio, however, all of a sudden my phone started buzzing with texts and calls.

"I heard what happened," a friend from Iowa texted.

"Do you want me to come up there?" asked another.

More details of my stalker had hit the mainstream media, and my friends, family, and fans were all finding out things I hadn't learned yet. Apparently my stalker's name was Robert. He had at one time been training for the Olympic rowing team, but a back injury shattered his athletic dreams and he became very depressed. He'd been attending the University of Florida, where he studied engineering. When he saw me on TV, he felt he was telepathically communicating with me through the TV set. In his mind, he concocted a full, complex relationship with me, even though we'd never spoken. Once our "relationship" had progressed far enough in his mind, he decided he would come to Los Angeles, where he knew I was appearing on *Dancing with the Stars* every week.

As this information seeped out to the public, I became even more frightened. One detail was particularly odd. Apparently the guy had been stopped by an Alabama police officer for a traffic violation on his way from Florida to California. But rather than trying to hide his mission, he told the cop all about how he was going to marry me. "I know it sounds a little bit crazy, but my intuition tells me that we're going to have a beautiful relationship together."

The paparazzi, who had already been pretty attentive to me at *DWTS*, swarmed ABC searching for me. When I came to and from rehearsal, reporters stuck microphones in my face.

"Are you scared?"

"Will you stay on the show?"

"What contact have you had with your stalker?"

Even if I managed to put the guy out of my mind for a few minutes, I couldn't escape the constant reminders at every turn. I didn't like suddenly being a "victim." I smiled on the outside, but on the inside, I was in knots.

One day on the set after the news broke, one of the other women on the show pulled me aside. "Hey," she said, "I wanted to talk to you." She had a very serious look on her face. All of my *DWTS* friends had been so kind, offering to stay with me or talk with me whenever I looked worried. I thought she was going to give me a hug and tell me she was sorry for what I was going through.

I was wrong.

"That was a brilliant move," she said to me in a low voice. "I was thinking of doing the same thing."

"What do you mean?" I asked.

"Of hiring someone to stalk *me*!" she said, as if it were the most obvious thing in the world. "You beat me to it!"

I looked around to see if I had a witness to this conversation, because I couldn't believe my ears. "You were thinking of doing what?"

"Look, I'm not judging you. You're getting great publicity," she said. "It's a smart move because I'm sure you'll get a lot of sympathy votes. I just wish I'd done it first!"

She was actually jealous I had a stalker. She thought we'd *planted* him and set up the whole story. The more people who heard about my situation, she figured, the more votes I'd get. In her mind, because she didn't have a stalker, she was at a serious disadvantage.

You're twisted, I thought, but I simply smiled and walked away. I realized that I just didn't understand this new world. In athletics, you spend countless hours in a gym, day in and day out, to gain skills and earn respect. If your name is known in the gymnastics world, you know it's deserved. But in Hollywood, some people are known for the drama, scandal, bad decisions, or (ideally) a combination of all three in their lives. Whoever sparks the most drama, after all, gets the most attention from the media. And that can translate into Hollywood's definition of success: fame *and* fortune.

I began to miss the gymnastics world even more. Los Angeles . . . well, it was about as far from elite gymnastics or West Des Moines as it could be. And even though I was doing well on *DWTS*, I began to get depressed, longing for time on a balance beam instead of on the dance floor.

It didn't help that everyone was expecting Mark and me to do an amazing Lindy Hop, since this dance involves all kinds of tricks and flips. Though the producers stressed that my gymnastics career wasn't a benefit to me in the normal course of the competition, the Lindy Hop was supposed to be different because it emphasizes physical strength and agility more than elegance. And so we went into rehearsals knowing that we had a good chance to get ahead of the rest of the pack—but also realizing we were facing a lot of pressure.

I tried to look at this challenge as a good distraction from the ongoing questions about my stalker.

Not only was I struggling with fear, but I was also lonely. While my parents had always been there for me—and I appreciated their concern more than ever during this scary time—I felt suffocated by my mom's constant (court-ordered) presence. I also felt awkward about the gigantic bodyguard conscientiously following my every move. I needed my space and a true friend who understood exactly what I was going through. It was like I had both too much and not enough company.

Everyone else on the show seemed to have a "significant other." Mark was dating someone very seriously; Chuck Wicks was dating his dance partner, Julianne Hough; and Ty Murray was married to Jewel, who was always watching him adoringly from the audience. During this dark time, I wondered if I'd ever find the right guy who would be there for me when I needed him.

One night when I was sitting all alone in my new, extravagant hotel room, I evaluated my life. Sure, I'd managed to accomplish a great deal in my short seventeen years. But what did my future hold? I sat down with a pen and paper and made a list of goals:

Gain independence
Find clarity on whether to go back to gymnastics or not
Go back to high school and earn my diploma
Become a happier, healthier person
Stay in contact with my friends more
Write more poetry
Always give 150 percent

There was something about putting my thoughts on paper that made me feel like I was more in control of my destiny. I shut the journal, turned out the light, and closed my eyes. Eventually, thoughts of my stalker subsided long enough for me to sleep.

When it came time to go out there and perform the Lindy Hop, I was determined to give it my all. Mark and I had chosen terribly cheesy outfits that we had thought looked good earlier in the week when we met with the designers. When we pulled them out on performance night, I had my doubts.

"What were we thinking?" I said to Mark, holding up my blue shorts and top, which had "Shark" written on it. Mark's costume was *much* worse—red shorts, complete with knee-high socks, a headband, and nerdy glasses.

"Come on," he said. "We're going retro!"

Retro or not, I felt ridiculous. And pressured. People who'd seen us rehearse earlier that week said we might pull off the best Lindy Hop of all time. And so, after we were announced, we danced with everything we had. We incorporated a lot of gymnastics into the routine, and the audience loved it. When we finished, they jumped to their feet and applauded!

Too bad the judges were less enthused about all the tricks. We dropped to fourth place. Apparently, however, the fans called in and voted for Team Shark, because we survived to dance another week.

Little did I know I was about to be scrutinized for a lot more than my two-step.

Lesson I've Learned

Be cautious when necessary, but don't allow anything to get in the way of your goals. Let them be your direction. After the stalker incident, so many people asked me, "Are you going to go home?" That would have been letting the stalker win, and I would have had to give up my dream. I refused to do that.

CHAPTER 24

LITTLE BULLETS

True beauty in a woman is reflected in her soul. It is the caring that she lovingly gives, the passion that she shows.
—*Sam Levenson*

LIVING IN CALIFORNIA and appearing on a reality TV show was a fun diversion after years of competitive gymnastics.

Even when Mark and I didn't score as well as we'd hoped, I was still having the time of my life. *DWTS* was filmed across the hall from *American Idol*, so we got to see a lot of celebrities. I remember meeting *Idol* judges Paula Abdul and Randy Jackson one night.

In early April, my friend Mitchel Musso invited me to go with him to the *Hannah Montana* movie premiere. Mom and I jumped in the car, happy to have an excuse to hit the local shops, which were a lot more fun (and expensive) than my hometown Target. There were racks and racks of gorgeous dresses, and I tried them on one after the other.

"Mom," I said, frowning as I looked in the mirror, "nothing fits well."

Eventually, though, I found the perfect one.

"Here it is!" I said to my mom as I came out of the dressing room. I twirled around in the bright yellow dress and felt like a movie star. I still felt that way when a limousine came to pick me up on the night of the premiere.

"Hey, guys!" I said, giving Mitchel a hug before he introduced me to his entire family . . . who were all dressed *completely in black.* It was like a Johnny Cash convention, and I showed up as Little Miss Sunshine. I looked a bit silly standing next to them in my bright yellow dress, but we all laughed about it.

Not long after, I settled into my seat to watch the movie, in which Miley Cyrus's character, Miley Stewart, has to choose between embracing her small-town roots or being totally swept up in her secret pop-star persona, Hannah Montana. As I sat there in the dark, I couldn't help but identify with her struggle.

I was just a Midwestern girl from a relatively small town in Iowa. Yet my life had become a whirlwind of hairspray, Spanx, gravity-defying shoes, and custom-made costumes. Gradually, I felt myself becoming more and more enamored with the lifestyle, the glitz, and the glamour. It was all so exhilarating—to be young and in Los Angeles and on TV. Plus, I was still enjoying my new freedom from endless training and dietary restrictions. Life was unimaginably fun.

But there was one little, nagging issue that I kept trying to push to the back of my mind. When I went shopping for a dress that day with my mom, those outfits didn't fit as well as they should have. And when I looked in the mirror, the reason was too obvious to ignore.

I had gained weight.

What was happening? I'd never been the person to ask, "Do these jeans make me look fat?" The advantage of being in gymnastics from age three on is that I never had to worry about my weight or staying healthy. Well, that's not *quite* true.

I've always been strong and very muscular, and my solidly built body was eventually honed into the perfect little bullet—one that could shoot through the air quickly and easily. Unencumbered by excess fat, I could turn, flip, and vault my way into America's living rooms and right into people's hearts. I'd been in great shape my entire life. But that doesn't mean I didn't worry about my weight. In fact, I thought about it all the time.

Why would someone so fit think about her weight so much? Gymnastics is all about pushing a body beyond its natural limitations in beautiful and sometimes unimaginable ways. The thrill of the sport comes when you break through expectations . . . when the crowd gasps . . . when your feet thud onto the mat in a perfect dismount. The less I weighed, of course, the higher I could push myself off the beam, off the vault, and through the air. It was just basic physics.

But beyond the simple science of motion is the art of perception. We weren't ranked based on who crossed the finish line first or who threw a discus the farthest. We were evaluated according to the judges' preferences. Did they like the long, lean lines of Eastern Europeans? Did they prefer shorter, stockier builds? As a gymnast, I knew that my appearance actually influenced the perceptions of the judges and, consequently, my scores.

It's no surprise that elite gymnasts have become significantly younger and smaller over the decades. At the 1964 Olympics, twenty-six-year-old Vera Caslavska won the all-around title. She was five-three and 121 pounds. Four years later, thirteen-year-old Olga Korbut showed up on the scene. She was four-eleven and weighed a mere 85 pounds. Gymnastics would never be the same. In 1976, the average size of a woman on the US Gymnastics team was five-three and 105 pounds. In 1992, it was four-nine and 88 pounds.

The smaller-is-better stereotype of the gymnast is a generalization that will never go away. But there's one problem: when a preschooler walks into a gym for the first time, holding her mom's hand, no one knows how tall she will grow to be. Slowly, the coaches and the competitions weed out the girls who grow too fast to compete with the smaller girls, but this takes time. That's why the sport is so fickle. For years, a young gymnast will practice and perfect her skills. But when her body hits puberty, she's likely to lose her competitive edge, and her gymnastics career may be over. That's one reason Chow has always said there is no way to look at a six-year-old—even a very nimble, flexible, and determined one—and predict how far she will go in the sport.

Still, gymnasts are taught that one way to turn their bodies into little bullets that will shoot through the air is by remaining thin.

My entire life, various people had said the same thing:

"You need to lose a few pounds," I was told.

"You shouldn't be eating," I heard constantly.

"Step on the scales," I was instructed.

The lighter I was, the happier everyone was with me.

So when I looked in the mirror at that Los Angeles shop, it wasn't the first time I'd looked at my body critically. It was the millionth time. When you're told as a young child that you are not quite light enough, it takes a toll on you in a way I doubt I'll ever truly be able to escape.

For example, I remember being convinced I was overweight at the Olympics. Maybe it was because I was around so many high-achieving athletes, or maybe it was the pressure of the competition. However, I think it probably had something to do with the messages all advancing gymnasts are exposed to.

Now when I look at pictures of myself during those Games, I think, *Wow! I look anorexic!* After all, I weighed less than ninety pounds and had only 6 percent body fat.

But in Los Angeles, my critical eye was no longer looking at imagined weight gain or the illusion of cellulite. Instead, I was looking at real pounds. Real weight. A real problem.

What happened?

Several things. First, when I was training, my coaches severely limited the amount of calories I could eat. For years, I was conscious of every piece of food I placed in my mouth. Whenever I "cheated"—by sneaking those dinner rolls and candy bars—I felt guilty and worried that it might hurt my next performance. When I was finally free from such hyper-regulation, and in a place like Los Angeles that has so much great food, it took me a while to figure out what a reasonable amount to eat looked like. Second, my activity level dropped considerably. Many times, celebrities go on *DWTS* because of the heavily touted weight-loss benefits. Over the course of the show many stars have dropped pounds like they were hot coals, commenting in their postshow interviews, "Well, I may have lost the mirror ball trophy, but I can see my waist again!" This is due largely to the fact that their sedentary lifestyles were jolted by the new activity regimen. We rehearsed several hours a day, which is a big increase from most people's level of activity.

As an Olympic athlete, I was used to so much physical conditioning per day that *DWTS* took my activity level down a few notches. When some of the celebrities arrived in Los Angeles and saw the training schedule, they groaned at how much we were expected to do. I, on the other hand, joked to my mom, "I think I might be the only person to go on the show and actually gain weight!"

Much to my dismay, my lighthearted comment was beginning to come true. In my journal one night I wrote, "I feel fat, out of shape, and down on myself. I want to know how to lose weight and lose it fast, but I don't know how. It's just frustrating when I feel and look bigger than everyone else on the show."

Hollywood, of course, is all about physical appearances.

Women aspire to the ideal body type of Taylor Swift or Angelina Jolie, even though for most women that look is difficult or even impossible to achieve. Add to that the reality that the camera adds ten pounds, and it's easy to understand the emphasis that is put on body weight.

Finally, and perhaps most significantly, I went through puberty right before filming began. Yes, I was seventeen. Yes, this is later than the average girl. However, athletic girls tend to go through puberty later than nonathletic girls. Some gymnasts even try to delay puberty as long as they can by eating as few calories as possible. Low weight and low body fat can artificially stave off puberty, perhaps extending an already short career.

Of course, as adolescent girls develop, they look less like bullets and more like hourglasses. Hourglasses aren't known for their aerodynamic properties. They sit on a shelf, are admired, and count down the seconds until time runs out. In fact, when puberty hits, time sometimes *has* "run out" for gymnasts whose bodies are simply no longer built for the sport.

I'd been in Olympic training and then went right into the rigors of the post-Olympic tour. Only afterward, when I was out of the intensive training, did my body begin to change. One week before I went on *DWTS*, I finally began to turn into a normal girl. Suffice it to say, if I had to choose the most ideal moment to compete in a dance competition, it wouldn't have been right when my body was undergoing so many changes.

Blogs, newspapers, and even magazines talked about my new physique, writing things like, "Shawn Johnson, Olympic athlete, is now 20 pounds overweight."

I read that headline on my computer screen one night and thought, *No! I'm just finally a normal girl!*

I've always somehow managed to have a pretty thick skin when it comes to weight criticism. I don't know exactly how I've been able to keep my head about it, though I know my parents had a lot to do with it. They always encouraged me to eat, and my eagle-eyed mom would notice if I pushed my plate away without having eaten very much. Both my mom and my dad constantly told me I was beautiful, too. With their support, I was able to shake off any criticism I received about my weight, and I avoided developing an eating disorder.

Success, of course, helped my confidence as well. People could criticize my weight all day long, but when I was the number one gymnast in the world, it was easy to shrug it off. I'd simply smile and think to myself, *I don't need to lose weight. I was just in the Olympics!*

However, when I was on *DWTS*, I was well out of my comfort zone. I wasn't doing very well—at least I didn't think I was—and was already incredibly insecure about dancing in front of people. The immense pressure of the show was multiplied by the fact that everyone seemed to have an opinion about my weight.

I wish I could say that, once again, I didn't let the critics get to me. I wish I could explain that I was so comfortable in my own skin that I ignored their barbs. But to be completely honest, it got to me. It still gets to me. I will forever have a complex about my size. Being told you need to lose weight when you are only ten years old sticks with you. It just does.

The coaches didn't harp on our diets because they were mean; they were intent on helping us reach our goals. They kept us working and readjusting our goals, just as drill sergeants push soldiers to their limits. Of course, we weren't soldiers. We were little girls. Just a year or two before my appearance on *DWTS*, I sometimes longed for the day when I would be free from the sport, when I could do whatever I wanted.

But now that I was out of the gym and in Hollywood, I still faced the same old challenges . . . plus some new ones.

Lesson I've Learned

Seek to become comfortable and confident in your own skin. You'll always be judged by somebody, but remember that God created each of us differently. So don't be afraid to be your own person.

CHAPTER 25

THE MIRROR BALL OF GLORY

I'm not in competition with anybody but myself.
My goal is to beat my last performance.
—*Celine Dion*

I LOOK RIDICULOUS, I thought as I pulled my suitcase behind me through the doors to LAX. We'd just wrapped up the live taping for week six of *DWTS*, and I still had thick makeup caked on my face. I was also wearing fake eyelashes and long hair extensions. What looks good on TV looks terrible in real life, and I felt a little silly rushing to catch my flight. Then again, I doubted this was the first time someone had raced through the Los Angeles airport looking overdone.

After the taping ended around 8 p.m. that Tuesday, I went to see Mark play with his band at The Grove for about twenty minutes. Then I got a car to the airport so I could catch the red-eye flight to New York, which took off at 11.

This is how I began one of the craziest weeks of my life.

I was headed to Manhattan to attend a prestigious awards ceremony for amateur athletes. The James E. Sullivan Award is known as the "Oscar" of sports awards and is older than the Heisman. Since 1930, it's been given to amateur athletes based on the qualities of leadership, character, and sportsmanship in all areas of life. The Sullivan Award isn't simply given to the person with the most accomplishments, but instead, it honors an athlete who has also shown strong moral character.

I was thrilled to have been nominated, but traveling to New York meant taking a break in my increasingly intense training with Mark. We were one of only seven couples remaining in the competition. As we progressed, my desire to win that mirror ball trophy grew exponentially. By this time, we were practicing five or more hours a day, six days a week, and learning a new dance every week.

Mark stayed in Los Angeles for a group dance rehearsal that we would have to perform the following week, and he texted me updates on what I was missing.

"You are so glad you are missing this," he texted in a fit of boredom.

I'd been nominated for the Sullivan Award the previous year and didn't even make the top one hundred. This year, I was going to the ceremony as a *finalist*, which was exciting.

When my mom and I arrived in New York around 7 a.m., I was already feeling nervous about the day ahead. Once I got to my hotel room, it took me a while to remove all the makeup and hair extensions from the previous night. When *Entertainment Tonight* came a few hours later to film a brief segment on me, I was supposedly "getting ready" for the event. Of course, I was already dressed and made up for the night by the time they arrived. I didn't want to be applying mascara for the cameras, only to clump some on my eyelids!

I was up against some amazing athletes that night. The finalists included the US Olympic men's 400-meter freestyle relay swim team, volleyball player Cynthia Barboza, North Carolina basketball player

Tyler Hansbrough, and my fellow gymnast Nastia Liukin. The ceremony was held at the New York Athletic Club, and I found myself happy to be back in the realm of athletics instead of Hollywood. The difference was noticeable.

When my name was announced, I was shocked. *There's no way,* I thought. The Sullivan is the biggest honor there is for amateur athletes. Plus, I was the first female gymnast to ever win. It was an amazing honor.

And my week wasn't over.

After the ceremony, we flew back to West Des Moines, where I would accept another award later in the week. Mark met me in my hometown so we could rehearse. While it was wonderful to reconnect with him, I was even happier to see my golden retriever, Tucker. We'd been separated for eight weeks, and it felt so good when he ran into my arms.

While I was home, Mark and I rehearsed many hours to make up for the time I'd been away. This was the first time I'd missed rehearsals, and I was worried it would affect our performance. That made me a little testy with Mark during rehearsals, but he was great about it. One of his nicknames for me was BOJ (which stood for "bundle of joy"), but that week he threatened to change the "J" because I wasn't being very joyful.

I was so glad Mark had come to Iowa to practice because that meant he could go with me to the CHARACTER COUNTS! benefit on Friday evening. Five hundred people gathered at the Hy-Vee Conference Center in West Des Moines to honor me with the Robert D. Ray Pillar of Character Award. After a video introduction, I walked up to the podium to the strains of ABBA's "Dancing Queen." Most people don't get honored in their lifetime as much as I got honored in that one week. It was very humbling.

When I accepted the award, I made a speech, and I could have sworn that Mark teared up. I was happy he was there. But the best part was getting to receive such an honor in my own hometown.

Everywhere I went that week, one question kept coming up: "Are you going to return to gymnastics?" People were probably just curious, but they had no idea how complex my feelings were on the subject or how much uncertainty that question caused inside me. However, I'd usually just smile and say that, after *DWTS*, I planned on returning to the gym and seeing how my body responded. People seemed satisfied with this, especially after I assured them that I probably *would* be back one day. I didn't tell them I feared it might not even be possible.

I hated to say good-bye to Tucker (not to mention my dad), but Mark and I had to go back to Los Angeles, where all of the last-minute preparations for the show took place. For two straight days, Mark and I were either rehearsing our individual dance or rehearsing the group dance with the other contestants. Our only breaks were spent sleeping or grabbing something to eat. On show day, I slept. That night, I was really nervous that my time away would affect my performance. Thankfully, it didn't. We scored 9-9-10.

I was glad that week went so well, because the next week we had to perform the samba, which I found very frustrating.

"We need to see some more personality!" Mark said. He must have told me that a thousand times.

I had the moves down, but Mark wasn't happy. "Those are the right steps," he said, "but we need to see more personality. I want it to *sizzle*."

As much as I tried, my dancing wasn't as elegant and feminine as he had hoped. That's when he brought in his mom, Shirley Ballas, who is also a world champion dance instructor. Though I was a little embarrassed that I needed so much extra help, I wanted to win the competition.

"You're swinging your arms like you're swinging a baseball

bat," Shirley told me. "You need to elongate your arms into more feminine movements." Then she performed my part of the samba flawlessly. She also emphasized that I really needed to show emotion. Apparently, judges notice whether you're "in character" and whether the dance is moving you.

"I've never seen anyone who had so much difficulty showing emotion," she said during rehearsal, "and I've taught a lot of people."

"I just don't know what to do," I said after hours of trying not only to learn my steps but also to make sure my face was right.

"Well, at this stage of the competition," she said, "you really need to change your cardboard image."

Cardboard?

As soon as she said that, I remembered the time I ran into a cardboard cutout of myself in the soft drink aisle at my local Hy-Vee. Apparently, the whole nation had been gawking at my "cardboard self" on TV.

What was wrong with me? Why couldn't I overcome my shyness? The day of the competition, I slept in and tried not to think about it. But eventually I had to wake up, walk out on that stage, and be judged.

The samba went well overall. But the judges, once again, said it wasn't quite enough. Still, we got a 10-8-9, which was a relief. However, I couldn't help but think that my heart couldn't take too much more of this roller coaster.

Thankfully, it didn't have to.

Only three weeks remained, and I focused like never before on dancing as well as I possibly could. And I seemed to be getting better. Every week I tried desperately to show more personality, until—finally—we reached the semifinals, where we had to perform the Argentine tango. For the first time we received a perfect score: 10-10-10! I was thrilled, and the judges cooed over how well I delivered the emotional content. We were in the finals.

The last episode of the show was a two-hour extravaganza. As it went on, I got more and more nervous as I watched from backstage. Lady Gaga performed in one of her flamboyant costumes, which provided enough of a distraction to make me forget for a few minutes that this emotional road was coming to an end. Each couple had to dance twice during the show, including one of the dances from earlier in the season. Mark and I chose the cha-cha.

I felt so much more comfortable onstage, and I could tell that I had improved. When I heard the judges' score—10-10-10— I breathed a sigh of relief.

The other dance we had to perform was the freestyle, which was my favorite of the season. There were no rules; it was simply a fun way to end the season. We received another perfect score.

In the end, the popular vote would determine the winner. After a very dramatic announcement, Melissa was voted off. She had scored third place in the show, and it honestly hurt me to see her step down. She'd been asked to join the show at the last minute to replace someone who'd been injured, and she'd done an amazing job!

Then, after all of these weeks of hard work, training, high heels, and fake eyelashes, it was finally time to find out who'd won. Gilles stood with his partner, Cheryl Burke, and I stood with Mark. Standing on that stage, I felt satisfied that I'd done the best I could. This would be the tightest outcome in the show's history, we were told. Apparently the winning team won by less than one percent of the vote.

"It's come down to this moment," Tom said.

"Gilles and Cheryl," he read and paused dramatically. "Gilles, you thrilled audiences from the first night of the competition with your consistently fantastic dancing. Did the viewers vote to give you the trophy?"

"Shawn and Mark," the host said. "Shawn, in the past few weeks, you've risen to the level of a true champion. Did the viewers decide to hand you the trophy? After eleven hard-fought weeks of competition, the winners and new champions of *Dancing with the Stars* are . . ."

It felt like forever that the host let the announcement hang in the air. My heart raced, and I tried to maintain a calm face. But when he said, "Shawn and Mark!" I felt nothing but jubilation.

Immediately, Mark embraced me and twirled me around. The next few minutes were a blur of confetti, hugs, the mirror ball trophy, and Mark repeatedly falling on the floor. I'd done it! I'd faced my fears and simultaneously managed to win *Dancing with the Stars*.

Finally, life could get back to normal.

Lesson I've Learned

Surround yourself with people who you know love you for who you are and want the best for you. Then don't be afraid to open your heart to them.

CHAPTER 26

LEARNING TO BE ME AGAIN

Cherish the journey. . . . When we do, we appreciate the process rather than the outcome. We realize that even in life's not-so-good moments we are exactly where we are supposed to be.

—*Unknown*

THE MIRROR BALL TROPHY wasn't the only souvenir I brought home from *Dancing with the Stars*. As our season wrapped up, I was given the option of purchasing the handmade, custom-designed costumes I had performed in. Each one had been cut and assembled by seamstresses from fabrics shipped from a dance company in Europe. Every rhinestone and sequin had been painstakingly sewn on by hand; every cut had been made to complement my body and our specific dance for that week. Even though it seemed a little extravagant, I couldn't resist the offer. I wanted to keep those costumes as a reminder of my time in Hollywood.

I'd had a lot of fun competing on *DWTS*, but the biggest upside was that I'd proved to myself that I could excel at more than just gymnastics. Whenever I opened my closet doors and caught a glimpse of my yellow-floral Chiquita banana ensemble or my black-and-white polka-dot dress with the hot-pink fringe, I was reminded that if I put my mind to it, I could do just about anything.

It took me a while to figure out that there was a downside to my *DWTS* experience: I'd developed a bit of a Hollywood attitude. I'd started feeling the need to look cute at all times in case the paparazzi showed up. I'd become comfortable with all the glitter, the rhinestones, the red-carpet movie premieres, the attention from reporters, and the TV cameras that followed my every move. Without realizing it, I'd been influenced by some of the celebrities I'd met, people I looked up to.

My parents emphasized repeatedly that I shouldn't let others' expectations color my own personality and behavior. But in spite of my upbringing, for a while I lost myself in California. The differences in my personality were subtle, but they were there. For example, I stopped listening to country music. With the exception of Chuck Wicks, the *DWTS* cast thought the crooning and the thick accents were absurd. They listened to hip-hop. I found myself skipping over the country tunes on my iPod in favor of the newer, "cooler" songs.

I also found myself being less patient when I was out in public. Did the woman in front of me really have to tell the cashier about every detail of her day? My Midwestern manners were falling by the wayside too. I realized I didn't automatically say "please" and "thank you" anymore.

When I was on the show, I felt like a princess in my custom-made garments and meticulously applied makeup. Like Cinderella at the ball, I enjoyed twirling around and having fun on the dance floor. However, even then I knew that the clock was ticking and that all of it would disappear soon enough.

I just didn't realize how suddenly the void would appear. One day I was basking in the congratulations and compliments that came from weeks of hard work; the next, I was back in West Des Moines without an immediate goal to shoot for. Even my friends seemed to have disappeared from my day-to-day life. The friends

I'd made in Hollywood obviously didn't follow me home to Iowa. Not only that, but now my high school friends were preparing to head off to college.

I'd returned to high school only once in the spring of 2009, to talk with my counselor. When I did, it was chaos. Valley High had over two thousand students—it's the largest high school in Iowa—and on the day I came back to campus, it seemed like most of them started running after me, asking for autographs, or swarming the doorways simply trying to get a peek at me. I couldn't even walk down the hallway to get to my locker without causing a stir.

Clearly, I couldn't return to school. So instead of spending the remainder of my senior year going to dances, gossiping in the halls, and agonizing over where to sit in the cafeteria, I spent it in front of my computer screen taking online classes.

The attention, I found out, wasn't isolated to teenagers at high school. Everywhere I went, people did double takes. Though I tried to camouflage my appearance, people weren't confused by the sunglasses and hat. After all, I was still less than five feet tall and had the same blonde hair seen by tens of millions of people during the Olympics and *DWTS*.

"Hey," people repeatedly asked, "aren't you the girl from *Dancing with the Stars?*"

That always surprised me because I had never expected the show to define me. "No," I wanted to say when I was feeling particularly down. "I'm the girl from the United States Olympic Team!" However, I did understand why people focused on the show. The Olympic gymnastics competition was broadcast for just a few hours over the course of a few days during the Games. *DWTS* came on twice a week, several hours a week, for three months. It made sense that I was more readily identifiable as a dancer, but it seemed as if the biggest milestone of my life had been pushed away.

The public attention wasn't all bad, of course. In fact, it was mostly very encouraging. Kind older people would tell me that I was like a beam of sunshine on the TV screen. Sweet little girls who aspired to be Olympic athletes would nervously offer me a pen and paper. I enjoyed spending time with the young gymnasts most of all. After all, not many years before I had been one of them and had idolized famous top gymnasts. I had wanted to know what their favorite color was and what they'd eaten for breakfast. I was sure that if only I could connect with and relate to those gymnasts, I might someday be just like them. So nothing was more gratifying to me than seeing that same light on a little girl's face as she approached me.

In fact, I was so thankful for everyone's unwavering support through all my experiences that I stopped for a short chat or an autograph whenever possible, no matter where I was.

Well, there was one glaring exception.

One afternoon, I was in the bathroom at the local mall. Suddenly, a hand emerged under the stall holding a piece of paper and a pen.

"Excuse me," I heard the voice echo through the bathroom from the next stall. "Do you mind giving me your signature?"

Even though I loved and appreciated my fans, a bathroom autograph was too much.

"Um," I responded, "I'm a little busy over here. No thanks."

I waited until I was sure she was gone before coming out of that stall!

In other circumstances, I overheard people talking about me. For some reason, people assumed increased flexibility on the balance beam meant reduced hearing at the grocery store. More than once I heard whispered conversations that went something like this:

"Is that Shawn Johnson?"

"No, it can't be. Shawn isn't that fat."

Everyone's mental image of me was as a sixteen-year-old pre-pubescent gymnast. I couldn't help but believe that the real me was quite a disappointment.

I understood. I disappointed myself, too. Even though I'd won four medals in the Olympics and a mirror ball trophy on one of America's most popular TV shows, I was adrift. Though the Olympics and *DWTS* were both challenging, I had felt alive in the midst of those competitions. Once they were over, there was nothing in my life to anchor me.

I was back in the hometown I loved, but it suddenly felt dark and heavy. Not only was I no longer a public high school student, I was no longer training. For all intents and purposes, that meant that I was no longer a gymnast. I was a former gymnast. A former Olympic champion. A former athlete. And now that the show was over, dancing had gone away too. After devoting so much of my life to those two activities, I felt as if I had nothing left.

Sure, all kinds of opportunities were offered to me—movie roles, appearances, endorsements—and I had no problem keeping busy. When I was at the 2009 Visa Championships, attending as a spectator for the first time ever, I remember a reporter asking me, "How great is it to be Shawn Johnson these days?"

I said what I think she expected me to say, which was that I was having the time of my life. However, the second part of my answer was a more accurate reflection of my feelings: "I can't wait for it to die down a little so I can sort things out."

Throughout 2009, I was asked over and over whether or not I planned to compete for a spot on the 2012 Olympic Team. At that point, I wasn't sure my heart was ready to commit to that. After all, I knew the tremendous physical, mental, and emotional toll that level of training took. I also knew I would give anything to once again experience the mountaintop emotions I had felt while competing at the Olympics. I couldn't deny feeling a sense of loss, either. I'd often said that gymnastics was my life, and now it was like a part of me had died.

It took a long time for me to get back into the rhythm of things.

I was determined to get back in shape, too, but I struggled with learning how to work out on my own, eat a healthy diet, and take care of myself. Physically and mentally, I was at the unhealthiest point in my life.

Thankfully, after a few months I realized that I was struggling in part because the smooth-talking, red-carpet-walking persona I'd adopted is not really who I am. Hitting a low forced me to learn how to be me again . . . away from the limelight. It wasn't always easy, and not everyone was happy to see me jump off my pedestal.

Lesson I've Learned

Take time to discover who you are as an individual, and don't let anyone else define you.

CHAPTER 27

SHAPING UP

To be nobody but yourself in a world that's doing its best to make you somebody else, is to fight the hardest battle you are ever going to fight. Never stop fighting.

—*e. e. cummings*

ONE NIGHT SHORTLY after I was back in West Des Moines, I went out on a date with a guy I liked. Once we were seated at our table in an elegant restaurant, I felt myself relax. I was enjoying a delicious meal and interesting conversation when, out of the corner of my eye, I saw someone nervously circling our table.

Don't do it. . . . Don't do it, I thought, while trying to maintain eye contact with my date. Eventually, the pacing woman got over her inhibitions enough to approach the table.

"I know I shouldn't be doing this," she said. "Sorry to interrupt your meal, but I just wanted to ask you . . ."

My dates were interrupted so frequently by people seeking autographs that I often felt like I was on a group date. Consequently, it was hard to get to know anybody in a real and meaningful way.

One guy seemed promising, though. We found a great place to eat, and none of the other diners seemed to notice that we were there. We talked about my life for a while, and then I asked about his family, work, and hobbies.

"Well, I actually like to watch gymnastics," he said.

"Really?" I took a bite of veggies. He hadn't mentioned even knowing about my gymnastics life before this moment.

"You know, I actually came to your welcome home event."

"Wow," I said, taking a sip of water. "You came to that?"

"Sure! I was there at Wells Fargo Arena," he said. "I was one of the thousands and thousands of people screaming for you."

"I thought you looked familiar," I joked.

Then he leaned in and said, "I've actually followed you through-out your whole career. I'm *such* a fan."

"Thanks," I said, before asking, "Well, who'd you go to the welcome home party with?"

"Oh, nobody," he said. "I just went by myself."

Suddenly, images of this single guy going to a welcome home party for a sixteen-year-old gymnast *by himself* seemed a little odd.

Uhhh, check please?

While I may not have known my next long-term goal, I have always known that one day I want to settle down, have children, and lead a peaceful life filled with playdates and family outings.

My parents had created that type of life for themselves. Once, when I was a kid, I asked Mom what she later told me was the most difficult question ever: "How will I be able to find someone as good as Daddy?"

My father is not a loud, opinionated man. He parents by example, which is probably the only way that really works. I've always been a daddy's girl, and Mom says we share some of the same charac-teristics. He's not afraid of hard work, loves adventure, and always has wise advice. As a kid, I couldn't imagine ever finding someone who was as well-suited for me as my parents are for each other.

I remember Mom telling me, "Don't worry. You'll find a man

who shares the same values we've taught you." Now that I was back in my hometown so many years later, I wondered if she was right. I'd gotten a hint of what such a relationship might be like when I was hanging out with Taylor in Beijing. While he remained a good friend, and one of the few who understood what I'd experienced at the Olympics, distance prevented our relationship from developing further.

Not only was I trying to rebuild my social life, but I also wanted to focus on getting back in shape. Through a former teammate from Chow's, I met a wonderful trainer—another former gymnast—who understood what my body had gone through over the past few years. Together we devised a healthy nutrition plan that would help me gradually lose the unwanted pounds. We went to the gym regularly, and I slowly began to reclaim my body. She was the perfect trainer for me. She knew exactly how to motivate me into a higher gear and exactly when to lay off a bit.

"Have you ever run a half marathon before?" she asked one morning at the gym.

"No," I responded. Gymnasts don't need the kind of stamina that comes from long-distance running, after all. The farthest I'd ever run at this point was around three miles. "But I'm in if you are!"

After training for several weeks, running shorter distances on the weekdays and longer runs on the weekends, we were ready for the 13.1-mile race. I was excited for a new physical challenge. How hard could it be?

When I met my trainer at the race, however, she took one look at me and frowned. "Are those new shoes?"

"Do you like them?" I asked, turning one foot to the side to show them off. I wanted to look cute for my big day.

"They're nice," she said. "But new running shoes will be stiff at first. I'm afraid that you'll get blisters."

Of course, I'd never thought of that. The race began well enough, but ultimately she was right. The pain started in my heel, and I tried to compensate by putting less weight on that leg. Then I got another blister on my other heel.

"I can't do it," I told my trainer. But she encouraged me to keep going.

"Come on," she said. "We can't walk."

The eleventh mile was the hardest. But finally, mercifully, I crossed the finish line and just collapsed. My legs and feet hurt terribly. After those thirteen miles, my whole body went into shock, and I sat down, exhausted.

"I can't move!"

But even though I didn't know if I'd ever get up again, inside I felt great! I was beginning to feel a little more like the old Shawn: competitive, athletic, driven. I could be all of those things without gymnastics, right?

Most days, I was thrilled to be free of the rigorous training schedule of my old life. I hadn't seen Coach Chow often, and I sometimes wondered how he was doing. I had heard he'd gotten an influx of new students after we returned from Beijing and was busy training more Olympic hopefuls.

I was glad to be back in shape in case I decided I wanted to return to gymnastics, but I wasn't ready to make that commitment yet.

Lesson I've Learned

Choose an exercise partner or a fitness program that will keep you from slacking off, move you along steadily toward your fitness goals, and yet allow you some breathing room when you need it.

CHAPTER 28

HOW GOD BECAME MORE REAL TO ME

Where there is great love, there are always miracles.
—*Willa Cather*

ONE DAY, MY TRAINER introduced me to Ryan, a redshirt foot-ball player for the University of Iowa. I learned he was in town to support his older sister, who was battling stage 4 non-Hodgkin's lymphoma. He'd come to offer encouragement and help her with her four kids. I immediately liked him, and it seemed reciprocal. After a Facebook mix-up (in which he sent a message to the wrong Shawn Johnson), we began hanging out: I went to his games, we hung out in Iowa City, and he even came to my mom's birth-day party.

One night, I had an idea.

"Why don't you come to West Des Moines? I'll take you out for a real date—my treat." Even though I love it when guys act like gentlemen by paying for dates, I sometimes feel bad when they're always expected to pay. He was a college student, after all.

The next week, he drove to West Des Moines, and I took

him to HuHot, my favorite Mongolian restaurant. It's a little loud and decidedly not romantic—in other words, it was perfect. We ordered our appetizers and drinks and then walked around to the grilling area to decide among the many food options. At this restaurant, the customers select vegetables—my favorite!—meats, and then sauces. We piled our bowls high, passed them to the chef, and watched as our food was prepared on a huge grill.

We ordered *a lot* of food—partly because Ryan is a big football player who needs to eat large portions, but mostly because I wanted to treat him to a nice evening. After we ate our meals, we ordered the cheesecake empanadas, desserts that look like ravioli but are actually filled with cheesecake.

Why not? I thought. Since I was paying, we just kept racking up the bill. When we got the check, I made a big show of grabbing it and handing the waitress my credit card.

"Remember," I said, "this is on me!" As we finished nibbling the last of the empanadas, I felt our date had been a resounding success. But just a few minutes later, the waitress sheepishly approached my side of the table.

"Miss Johnson," the embarrassed waitress said, slipping my credit card into my hand. "There seems to be a problem with your card."

"It didn't work?" I asked. But then I could tell by her expression that she was trying to help me save face.

"Oh," I smiled at Ryan. "Don't worry. I have another credit card in my car."

I ran outside and scrounged through the console and the glove compartment for another credit card. I found sunglasses, an old parking ticket, and some stale gum, but nothing that would help me get out of this humiliating situation. I grabbed my phone and hoped Mom or Dad would answer.

"Mom!" I said into my phone. "My credit card was declined!"

"What?" she asked.

"I *may* have forgotten to pay on time or something," I said, realizing that every second spent in the parking lot was making it more awkward for Ryan. "What should I do?"

"I don't think I can get there in time," she said.

"He's never going to go on another date with me!" I cried into the phone, finally slamming the door shut and hanging up.

When Ryan saw me slink back into the restaurant, hanging my head in shame, he smiled and gave the waitress his credit card. I figured I'd never see him again.

Surprisingly, Ryan didn't stop calling after I stuck him with the bill at HuHot. We kept hanging out, and our friendship grew. After my time in Hollywood, Ryan helped bring me back down to earth and made me realize that I'm a Midwestern girl at heart. Like me, he comes from a close-knit, physically active family. My parents have always loved nature and the outdoors, and his family does too. They own a cabin on a lake in Iowa, and Ryan loves to hunt and fish. As a college football player, he is committed to athletics and a healthy lifestyle, just like I am.

Early in our relationship, I let Ryan read a few of my poems. One day, he jokingly told me that he would know I really cared for him only if I wrote a poem about him. In fact, as our friendship deepened, that's exactly how I chose to express my feelings:

It's strange how guys come in and out of your life,
always hoping they'll be Mr. Right. . . .
They'll change you and make you want to cry.
And never really understanding why,
you'll notice that with each one you seem to change,
adapting to interests so you seem the same;

acting for some and hiding for others,
just wanting to be accepted and love each other.
But it's the ones that end wrong and seem right from the start
that change you the most and break you apart.
You act like a stranger and look in a mirror
and don't even recognize who's standing there.

Unlike the guys I'd dated who were drawn to me because of what I'd done, Ryan was interested in the person I was inside. As a result, I felt I could relax around him and be myself:

I don't know where he came from or how long he will stay,
but I promise that I can safely say,
I am now happy, and it is the first time in a while.
And around him it's my heart that seems to smile.

In the summer, Ryan moved to West Des Moines to be closer to his sister and her husband. He took care of their four kids, mowed their grass, and shopped for groceries. Though I couldn't do much to help, I volunteered to take the kids to the movies and out for ice cream. I thought the extra attention might help distract them from the day-to-day reality of their mom's sickness.

Anything I did for those kids was nothing compared to what Ryan's sister did for me. I never saw her complain. When I went to Omaha with the family for her chemotherapy treatments, everyone seemed to be faithful, patient, loving, and—most of all—prayerful. People from their church and neighborhood provided a hot dinner every night. A cleaning service donated their time to dust and vacuum her home, since she wasn't able to follow her four young children around with a mop. Ryan's parents sometimes brought the kids to their home for a week.

I never sat down with Ryan or his family to have an in-depth theological discussion. But I learned a great deal about God's love by witnessing Ryan's family and their church wrap their arms around his sister during this terrible time. It was much more powerful than any sermon could be.

When her cancer went into remission, I considered it a miracle.

Ryan's mom is the director of spiritual formation at a church, and I think she understood right away that I was searching to understand and grow in my faith. For my birthday she gave me a daily devotional that included a prayer and a Scripture reading for every day of the year. Each morning as I opened that book, I read about God's goodness and provision. She gave the same book to Ryan. Though we were two hours apart, reading the same devotional each day kept us connected.

As Ryan and I talked about our faith, God became more real to me. Maybe this sense of God's presence was just a natural by-product of the way I had been raised. My parents had faith and were absolutely rock-solid about doing what is right, but I realized that I could also learn something from Ryan and his family. Like my parents, Ryan's family didn't preach to me. However, as I spent time with them that summer, I noticed that they just oozed peace, joy, and love, even though they were living through the worst time of their lives. They were always positive and taught me to leave everything to God, because when we try to manage everything on our own, it's too much for us to handle. That's when we realize that God is the one who's in control and that he does a better job of it than we do.

As I reflected on the Bible, my faith began to deepen. When I was a little girl, I loved going to vacation Bible school at Lutheran Church of Hope, and my parents and I had attended services there occasionally as I was growing up. Now we began going more regularly. During a service in the church's early days, my mom recalls the pastor tearfully confiding that he wasn't sure if the church was going to succeed. Today it is the largest church in the city.

Lutheran Church of Hope's size is not what appeals to me, though. Instead, it is the feeling I get whenever I attend on a Sunday morning. No matter how many services I've missed because of out-of-town engagements or training, when I return I feel like I never left. Pastor Mike and the leaders welcome everybody—from the polished professional who comes in a suit to the harried mom who shows up in sweats.

My church is a safe place for someone like me who grew up feeling embarrassed because I had no idea who my friends were talking about when they mentioned people in the Bible. The church leaders don't expect anyone to recite names and dates; their concern is that each person grows in faith and in love for one another and for Christ. They want us to understand that God's love for us doesn't depend on anything we might do.

Ironically, I had come home from *Dancing with the Stars* convinced that I needed to find a new identity for myself. Thanks to my parents, Ryan's family, and my church, I realized that my true identity comes from something other than my accomplishments and that lasting happiness will never be found in another medal or trophy. True and lasting joy, I discovered, is the by-product of living in the countercultural way described by the apostle Paul two thousand years ago: "Always be humble and gentle. Be patient with each other, making allowance for each other's faults because of your love" (Ephesians 4:2).

This type of life might not get much airtime in the glittery, highly choreographed world of Hollywood, but by early 2010, I was discovering that my contentment began and ended with simple things like faith, hope, and love.

Lesson I've Learned

Now that I've opened up my heart, I've seen what good can come from finding someone who loves you for who you are—not for titles, fame, or glamour. Nothing brings more peace and joy than being loved for who you are.

CHAPTER 29

WIPEOUT

We could never learn to be brave and
patient if there were only joy in the world.
—*Helen Keller*

GYMNASTS AREN'T supposed to ski. Just as a surgeon's hands are
important to his or her livelihood, gymnasts' legs and knees allow
us to explode off the vaults and pull off intricate beam maneuvers.

Even though Mom and Dad never wanted me to feel imprisoned
by my sport, I studiously avoided the slopes. However, once the
Olympics were behind me, I convinced Mom and Dad into taking
me skiing so I could finally enjoy the feeling of flying down a mountain on fresh powder. When we loaded up Dad's truck and headed to
Colorado for Christmas 2008, I couldn't have been happier.

I loved everything about skiing—the warm jackets, the cozy
gloves, the cool goggles—and, of course, the adrenaline rush. After
a couple of runs down the bunny slope, I was ready for a more
challenging course. Pretty soon I was doing black diamonds. I was
as daring on the slopes as I'd been on the beam.

In January 2010 my parents arranged another ski trip to

Colorado to celebrate my upcoming eighteenth birthday with some family and friends, including my cousin Tori; Ryan; Ryan's best friend, Brandon; and my close friend Alice. I was thrilled to celebrate this milestone birthday with such a fun group of people.

Once we arrived in Beaver Creek, I was delighted at how picturesque the setting was. The mountains seemed to embrace the little villages nestled into the slopes. Beaver Creek has everything you could hope for in a ski resort—ice-skating rinks, a museum, restaurants, and bonfires everywhere you go. S'mores kits are available on every corner, so you can enjoy a snack while warming up near a fire.

We skied every day on the wonderfully fresh, beautiful snow. It was relaxing and fun. After all those years of being judged, I loved simply being on the slopes with friends and family. At the same time, it's always been hard for me to participate casually in physical activities. I'm so competitive that I have to inject a little rivalry into things. I raced my dad down the easy hills to see who could make it to the bottom first. My mom kept shouting, "What are you guys doing?"

After a run, we'd meet at the bottom of the slopes, where men in white chef hats and aprons walked around with trays of warm chocolate chip cookies. One evening we went ice-skating at the rink in Beaver Creek Village, the main social hub in town. Ryan and I rented skates and headed out onto the ice, hand in hand.

Because my dad was a hockey player, he taught me how to skate. I'm good on skates, but I don't glide around the ice with the elegance of an Olympic figure skater.

"You skate like a big hockey player," Ryan said as I was moving across the ice-skating rink like some sort of brute. We both laughed. I couldn't imagine life being any sweeter than this.

As a gymnast, I was used to ignoring pain and training through it. So when my shins began feeling sore that week, I didn't think much about it and kept skiing. By our last day at Beaver Creek, however, the pain had gotten so bad I didn't know if I could even go down the slopes.

"Don't ski," Ryan said to me that morning. "I can teach you how to snowboard. That shouldn't hurt your shins as much."

"No, no," I assured him. "You don't have to babysit me. I want you to have fun."

Looking back on it, I realize I was being stubborn. But I didn't want to miss out on anything. So I put on my gear and headed out to the slopes.

For several hours, we skied, laughed, and had a great time. My shins even felt a little better. We got to the last run, and the entire group stood at the top of the mountain looking down at the path, which split off in two different directions. On one side there was a challenging black diamond; on the other side, a more forgiving green run. Everyone wanted to go the black diamond route, but I finally made a decision that made sense.

"No, I'm super tired, and my shins are still hurting," I told them. "I'm just going to take it easy and go down this one."

I watched as my friends and family skied down and disappeared behind the tall aspens. I stood at the top of the mountain for a while. I wanted to remember this moment. I took pictures, soaked in the breathtaking scenery, and enjoyed the last minutes I had on the mountaintop. Very few skiers were on the slopes at that time, so nobody was around when I finally took off alone.

About halfway down, something unexpected happened.

I assume I hit a patch of ice, because I lost control. As I fell, the safety release on my ski didn't work. My ski got caught in the snow, and I rolled over my knee. That's when I heard a pop.

I slid down the slope, leaving my gear behind. My glasses flew off. My hat came off and landed about ten feet away. My poles were strewn around and stuck in various drifts. If onlookers didn't know any better, they might have thought I was holding a ski gear yard sale. Finally I stopped sliding and came to a complete stop. I sat there for a while, helpless and silent. It hadn't really dawned on me that I'd hurt myself. I didn't yet realize that the pop I'd heard was a sign that my life was about to change.

I sat there for ten minutes or so before a snowboarder reached me. On her way down, she collected my things, one by one.

"Are you okay?" she asked, handing me my gloves.

"Yeah, I'm fine," I said. "I'm just going to sit here a little longer." She looked at me suspiciously. "Are you sure?" she asked.

When I reassured her, she got up and snowboarded down the slope. I watched her until she became a small dot at the bottom of the mountain. That's when I saw my whole group, who had just made it down their black diamond.

"Hey, guys!" I yelled with as much volume as I could muster. "Up here!"

They had been scanning the people at the bottom of the mountain, looking for me. They figured I would ski fast just to get to the cookies first. Alice heard my voice and smiled when she saw me.

"Are you okay?" she yelled, waving.

Though I wasn't sure of the extent of my injuries, I didn't feel right. "No!" I yelled back. And with that one syllable, I could see everybody begin to panic. Even from that distance, it was obvious they were worried.

My dad took off his skis and began walking up the mountain. As soon as he got to me, I started crying. There was something so comforting about having him there by my very cold side.

"I hurt my knee," I said.

"Okay, let's call somebody," he said. "We can put you on a stretcher and get you help down there."

"No!" I protested. "I'm never going to ride down on one of those things!" Ryan was at the bottom of the slope, and there was no way I was going to let him see me being carried down the mountain on a stretcher. Even though I suspected something was wrong, I figured if I ignored it everything would be fine. That's why I assured my dad—and myself—that all was well. Then, to prove my point, I actually skied down what was left of the mountain. When I got to the bottom, however, I couldn't hide my emotions. I just bawled. It took me a while to shake it off and regain my composure.

Ryan looked very concerned.

"Oh, I'm fine. I'm fine," I assured him. I took off my skis and my boot and rolled up my pant leg. "See?"

When we looked at my leg, we were both surprised that it was already black and blue. Ryan offered to take me to the lodge.

"No, I'm fine," I repeated, jumping up and down on my knee to prove it. "See? I'm okay," I said, as much to myself as to him. "It's just a sprain; I'll be fine."

But in the back of my mind, I worried that something might be seriously wrong.

PART 4

Coming Back

One day at a time,
the clock keeps going;
the world keeps turning.
I keep dreaming, hoping, praying
that the answer will come to me.
You look, you search, you never find
that little sign you're looking for, because,
like a butterfly,
the more you look, the more it hides.
But turn around and you'll see:
it flies to you so gracefully.

CHAPTER 30

EVERYTHING CHANGES

You must do the thing you think you cannot do.
—*Eleanor Roosevelt*

WHAT I REMEMBER most about the moments after I heard my knee pop is not the pain. Instead, it was a not-yet-fully-formed fear that flashed through my mind: Could I have lost the opportunity to return to gymnastics? Until that moment, I'd always had the option. When people asked me if I planned to train for a spot on the 2012 Olympic team, I could assure them I was considering it.

During the first few weeks after I returned home from Colorado, I'd think about my future as I drifted off to sleep. I was tempted by the idea of a normal life. College. A long-term relationship uninterrupted by practice and meets. Time for other activities. But then I'd think of gymnastics, and I'd feel a pang of longing. Was my knee injury ending my gymnastics life forever? Would I never know if I had more to give the sport that had given me so much?

That may be why I tried so hard to convince Ryan, my parents, and most of all, myself that my injury wasn't serious. Also, I'd spent

most of my life in a high-impact sport in which knee injuries, ten-
donitis, fractures, and strains are common. Gymnasts don't cater to
pain and sometimes don't even acknowledge injury.

I was no longer a gymnast, but this attitude had been ingrained
in me for so many years that I refused to go to the doctor. Anytime
someone told me I should get a professional to look at my knee,
I shrugged it off. "Oh, it'll be fine," I said. "It'll heal."

But I knew—and everyone else knew—that something was
wrong. For example, when I jogged I had to run in a perfectly
straight line. If my body moved even slightly sideways, I'd collapse
in pain. My trainer watched this and gently suggested that I see
an expert.

"I just want you to go see one of my physical therapists," she
said, fully aware of my stubborn streak. She'd heard me repeatedly
refuse to see a doctor, so she offered the therapist as a middle step.
She knew if she could get me to a professional, he'd at least talk to
me honestly.

But even the physical therapist realized he would need to handle
my stubbornness carefully. After examining me for only a few
minutes, he knew what was wrong. However, he was aware that if
he suggested there was a problem—a real problem—I'd walk out
of there and never seek medical attention again. "Shawn, I really
encourage you to go get an MRI," he said diplomatically. "Let's
just make sure nothing's wrong."

My orthopedic doctor also knew what was wrong as soon as
I walked in. But even he didn't let on until after I'd agreed to the
MRI. "Worst-case scenario," he said, "you've got some sort of little
tear that'll heal on its own. Let's get in there and see what we're
dealing with."

In the midst of my doctor and PT visits, I kept doing my normal routine—running, working out, and fulfilling commitments
to sponsors. I especially enjoyed the photo shoot for some "Got

Milk?" ads. Who hasn't seen someone they recognize wearing that iconic milk mustache? And I definitely didn't want to forfeit my spot as a torchbearer for the 2010 Winter Olympics. On my eighteenth birthday, I carried the torch down the streets of Calgary as Canadians lined the streets. Holding that torch up high as I made my way past the cheering crowd definitely ranks as one of my favorite Olympic memories.

Once I was home again, I went right in for the MRI. After the procedure, my doctor told me he would call me with the results later that day. I left the doctor's office feeling on edge. I had finally gotten to the place where I actually wanted to know what was wrong. I wanted to be able to validate the pain I was feeling, but at the same time I hoped any damage wasn't irreparable.

As soon as I got in the car, I took out my cell phone and dialed a familiar number, one I hadn't called often in the last few years.

I felt the tears begin to fall even before my call was answered.

"Hello, Shawn!"

"Could I meet with you at the gym?" I asked.

Chow sounded a bit surprised but pleased to hear from me. "Sure. Do you want to set up a time to meet next week?" he asked.

"Actually, could I come by right now?" I'm sure Chow could hear me sobbing into the phone.

"Of course," he said.

The drive to Chow's Gymnastics felt as natural as if I'd never stopped going there to train every day. But I was nervous as I walked into the gym, and I was afraid of Chow's reaction to what I planned on saying. Still, I thought I had no choice but to lay everything out there.

Once we were seated in his office, I said, "Coach Chow, I want to come back. I miss gymnastics." Then I told him how I injured my knee and how, in the moment I heard something pop, I immediately thought of gymnastics.

Gymnastics is such a demanding, unforgiving sport, and no one understands that better than Chow. As I broke down in tears, I prepared myself for a negative reaction. What if Chow didn't want to take me back? I had walked away from everything, and I was asking him to make a big commitment by overseeing my training again—especially now that I had injured my knee.

Chow surprised me.

"Okay, Shawn," he said. "Just calm down."

He told me to look at this injury as a blessing. "You've been stumbling around during the past two years," he said. "You've been traveling and working. Now you have a chance to figure out what you want to do with your life once and for all."

"Do you think I can come back from this?" I asked hesitantly.

"It'll be much more difficult—not just mentally, but physically," he said. "You come back after you hear from your doctor. As you start training again, little by little, we'll see how you feel and if you're still enjoying it. It is going to take time and a lot of work, but if you are willing to commit to it, I'm willing to work with you."

It wasn't probable, but it was possible. That's all I needed, and his encouragement was music to my ears!

"Plus, I can see in your eyes that you still have a heart for the sport," he said. "Go get your knee fixed first and then come back."

Chow gave me hope . . . just like old times.

A few hours later, I returned home and ran upstairs to see my mom. I plopped down on her bed as she was getting ready in the adjacent bathroom. The conversation began just like any other talk we'd ever had, as we filled each other in on our plans for the day. That's when I casually asked, "So . . . has the doctor called with the results from the MRI yet?"

"Yeah, I heard from him," she said. I couldn't see her, since she was still in the bathroom putting on her makeup. But I knew from her voice that she wasn't telling me everything.

"Well?" If the problem was minor, she would have told me immediately. I almost had to force myself to ask her, "What did he say?"

She came into the bedroom and looked at me. "Well," she said, "you tore your ACL."

My heart sank at the three letters: ACL. Anterior cruciate ligament. The bone structure of the knee joint, I would learn, is formed by the femur, the tibia, and the patella. The ACL is one of the four main ligaments connecting the femur to the tibia. Like a tear in the Achilles, a torn ACL is an injury no gymnast ever wants to have.

Especially me. In a sport notorious for broken bones, I'd never had one. I'd never even had surgery before. My worst injuries were sprains or strains, little annoyances that didn't keep me from practice. Even my stress fracture hadn't kept me out of the gym for long. I was the fearless kid who flipped out of her crib, jumped off the kitchen counter, and fell off the monkey bars. I somehow always landed on my feet, with only scrapes and bruises to show for it.

How could this happen *to me*? I had always thought of myself as tough and unbreakable. Suddenly, as I sat on the bed, I realized I wasn't invincible.

"He said there's some other damage in there that needs to be fixed too," she gently added. "You need surgery."

Immediately, I started to cry. I was afraid to go under the knife, and I blamed myself for what I'd done. I don't even think I said a word to her as she matter-of-factly explained what needed to happen next.

Mom sat down on the bed and pulled me toward her. "You know, it's fine. Everything happens for a reason."

This is the same phrase, the same comfort she offered to me as a child when I faced minor disappointments. And here she offered it up again, with the same calming reassurance.

"For some reason, this was supposed to happen," she explained. "I bet you would have torn your knee doing something else that day, had you not gone skiing." As strange as it may sound, her words made me feel a little better.

Lesson I've Learned

Everything happens for a reason. Let that help you keep perspective in the hard times. Try to find the good in everything that happens—it's usually there somewhere.

CHAPTER 31

THE SURPRISE ANNOUNCEMENT

You can't put a limit on anything. The more you dream, the further you get.
—Michael Phelps

THE WORST PART OF MY INJURY, my doctor told me, was that I'd torn my meniscus. If I'd torn only my ACL, I could have been back on my leg in a mere four weeks. Unfortunately, I had what he called the "terrible triad." This meant I'd torn my anterior cruciate ligament, medial collateral ligament, and the meniscus. Always an overachiever, I'd managed to injure all three at once.

Before undergoing surgery, I had one more commitment to fill. My dad and I headed back to Canada, this time to Vancouver for the Winter Olympics. I was there as an ambassador for McDonald's Champion Kids program, which was created to encourage kids to be physically active. Several days after the opening ceremonies, we headed home so doctors could operate on my knee.

The surgeons took part of my hamstring off and attached it to my ACL to make a new ligament. When it was all over, I had stitches, darts, and a pin in my knee. They warned me to make sure it was completely non-weight-bearing for *eight weeks*.

In those first days of recovery, I realized that Chow had been right. I had been on such a roll since the Olympics—so caught up in the chaos of traveling to appearances and considering new opportunities—that I never had time to take a step back and think about what I wanted to do next. The injury gave me the time to really consider my options. Gymnastics was the path I saw to help me get healthy again and get my life back on track.

As I recovered, I developed a new daily routine. I started with three hours of school, followed by a quick lunch, three hours of therapy, a workout, homework, and then rest. My workouts had to evolve to accommodate the weakness in my knee. I couldn't run; however, I did upper-body exercises, swimming, and eventually even cycling. On some days, I swam four miles with a float between my knees. While my upper body got to be crazy strong, my legs were a whole different story. One of my thighs felt like a marshmallow.

At first I struggled with my crutches, but later I got pretty good at maneuvering on them. Using them gave me new empathy for anyone with any sort of disability. Though most people are kind and considerate, others . . . not so much. I was always shocked at how people sometimes looked at my crutches as an inconvenience *to them*.

"Miss, you can't take those on board," one flight attendant told me because she didn't know where to store them on the plane.

I had no idea what she thought I would do without them—I guess she expected me to hop down the aisle. *It could be so much worse*, I tried to remind myself as I attempted to keep my sense of humor about it all. I knew I couldn't guarantee any sort of a comeback, but I never dreamed how terribly I'd miss just doing a normal workout. During those weeks of recovery, I did a lot of soul-searching and praying.

Just over a month after my surgery, I had another first: I gave my first formal speech at the University of South Florida. Though I was incredibly nervous before my talk, the students seemed very receptive as I encouraged them to be true to themselves and follow their dreams. Only a few days later, I spoke to several hundred Girl Scouts in Cedar Falls, Iowa. I told the girls how I had struggled to fit in when I was younger and how my passion, gymnastics, had helped me find my place. Then I asked the crowd to raise their hands if they knew any "mean girls." Just about every hand went up.

"I'm sorry to tell you it doesn't go away," I said. Then I shared the lesson my mom had taught me: you can't change what others say about you, but you can change the way you respond to criticism and insults.

I was energized by the girls' enthusiasm as I spoke. I enjoyed even more the chance to talk with the girls one-on-one. While I was busy with the organizers, several teenage girls came up to my mom. They asked her to tell me how much it meant that I'd shared my story. They, too, struggled to fit in, so they felt I'd really connected with them.

After my eight weeks of recovery, I went back to Chow's Gym ready to resume gymnastics training. It was a little surreal to be training under a gigantic poster of myself from the Olympics, which hung on Chow's wall. However, the poster served as a daily reminder of what was and what could be again. It helped me stay focused, even when six-year-olds were running circles around me.

At first I thought life would slow down, but before I could really focus on training, I needed to fulfill a number of commitments. Two were particularly meaningful. On May 4, I was back in the Hy-Vee Hall in Des Moines speaking to seven thousand fourth-, fifth-, and sixth-graders from across Iowa as part of a CHARACTER COUNTS! event.

The atmosphere was energetic and uplifting as the excited kids screamed and cheered for me. I stood on the stage and soaked it all in. The event was called Exercise Your Character, and I talked to them about setting goals and not letting people dissuade them from reaching for their dreams. I told them the story about how a coach at my first gym told my mother I had no talent. I told them not to listen to those who tell them they aren't able to pursue their dreams.

Then, just after I'd finished speaking, a kid yelled out, "Are you going to the 2012 Olympics?" It seemed like the entire arena went silent.

Out of nowhere, something just clicked inside me. And right there in front of every camera covering the event, I said, "About London, everybody, I don't know if you know this, but I am going to give it a shot! I'm going to go for it!"[4] As everyone clapped and cheered for me, I walked down off the stage and thought, *Oops!*

Within seconds, every phone seemed to be ringing. I had really stirred something up. I quickly texted Sheryl: "I just announced in front of 9,000 that I'm going to try for London." I knew my parents would be thinking, *What!?* Chow hadn't even told me I could return to training yet, let alone make a comeback. On top of that, Sheryl would have wanted to orchestrate such an announcement.

I saw Donna Tweeten, a member of Hy-Vee's marketing team. She was smiling and holding out a phone to me. "Sheryl is on the phone. She wants you to know she's not upset, but she would like to talk with you right now."

Sheryl told me she'd already gotten a call from *Sports Illustrated* for confirmation that this rumor was true. My mom had gotten calls from reporters, and she responded in all honesty, "I had no idea she was going to announce this today!" Though this wasn't how I'd planned to tell the nation of my comeback, it was the perfect way. I spoke from the heart, and it just bubbled out of me.

A few weeks later, I was back in Beijing for the grand opening of Woodward Beijing, a 425-acre extreme sports arena and educational facility. The original Camp Woodward had been founded in

Pennsylvania in 1970, largely as a gymnastics training institute. By 2010, it had spread to five locations in the United States and, now, one in Beijing. I went along to represent gymnastics.

While there, we toured the National Indoor Stadium, the arena where I had competed in the 2008 Olympic Games. Though the gymnastics equipment wasn't set up, walking down into the stands and onto the floor was emotionally overwhelming. Time seemed to stop, and I felt like I was reliving every moment of the Games. The people touring with me noticed that I was close to tears, and they all stood around watching me and waiting. "You have no idea how hard this is," I told them.

To this day, I have never watched my Olympic performances from start to finish. It's just too emotionally taxing. Though I had been nervous about our visit to the stadium, wondering how I'd feel, I was still unprepared for the intensity of my response.

While my visit to Beijing reminded me of the incredible joy I'd felt at the Games, shortly after I returned home I had to deal with something I'd tried to push to the furthest recesses of my mind: my stalker.

About fifteen months had passed since Robert O'Ryan was apprehended after jumping a studio fence, but he was finally having his day in court. This meant I was about to have mine, too. My family and I had to go to the Los Angeles Criminal Courts Building to face him.

I hated the idea of having to be in the same room with that man. I wasn't sure I had the emotional strength to face him. Yet, when the day came, I forced myself to walk into that courtroom.

O'Ryan claimed to be insane, and I believed him. In a tape of an interview with police that was played in court, he testified that he heard voices in his head. He claimed this allowed us to begin communicating telepathically while I was in Beijing at the Olympics.

Because O'Ryan had waived his right to a jury trial, Judge

Michael Pastor, a well-regarded Superior Court judge who handled the most serious criminal cases in LA, would hand down a decision.

I spent twenty-three minutes on the witness stand, and it was one of the most difficult things I've ever had to do. The worst part came when the prosecutor laid the items officers found in O'Ryan's car on a table in front of me: two loaded guns, a knife, a club, and a bulletproof vest. I'd read about these items in the papers, but seeing them made me lose my breath.

When I looked at my mom, she was sobbing.

The judge found O'Ryan guilty of felony stalking, burglary, and two concealed weapons violations and ordered him to be sent to a California mental institution.

After I testified, I hugged my mom. "I thought we were going to be tough!" I said.

"I just felt so sad when I heard you testify about how scared you were," she cried, "and I couldn't be there to fix it for you."

I returned home, grateful that this chapter of my life had ended and I could again put all of my energy into training.

Lesson I've Learned

Don't let anything hold you back from following your heart and taking a leap of faith. Even if you're the only one who believes in the direction you want to take, you have the power to make it happen.

CHAPTER 32

A NEW IDENTITY

There are no limits. There are only plateaus, and you must not stay there, you must go beyond them.
—*Bruce Lee*

DECIDING TO TRY for a comeback did simplify life in some ways. It meant postponing college and canceling events on my celebrity schedule. Once again, my activities would need to fit around the training I did six days a week. Casual observers might have assumed that life had reverted pretty much to what it was in 2007 and early 2008, when I was gearing up for my first Olympic bid.

Actually, so much was different this time around. My injury had left me with about 40 percent of the capability I'd had two years earlier, making my goal of a comeback seem pretty audacious. I also had to deal with self-doubt—something I never really battled the first time around. As an athlete himself, Ryan understood and supported me through those difficult days. Though I was in West Des Moines and he was at school in Iowa City, we stayed in frequent contact and visited each other on weekends whenever we could.

Once I returned to the gym, I felt an urgency to get back into full training mode as quickly as possible. I put rehab on the back burner, despite Chow's attempts to move me forward at a reasonable pace. Though I trained more hours than I had before Beijing, he made sure my workouts were less intense and limited my time working out on the hard floor. Still, I pushed myself every day, whether or not I was tired, because I was frustrated by how slowly I seemed to be progressing.

I made my first trip back to the Karolyi ranch for a US National Team training camp in November, though I wasn't yet doing full routines. Two years is an eternity in gymnastics, so I was worried. Would I still fit in? Would I be accepted? It turned out to be an amazing experience. I loved seeing the team coaches and the other gymnasts. The best part, though, was being warmly welcomed back by Martha.

As encouraged as I was by my time in Texas, I returned home to a difficult reality: my knee had become quite painful again. Apparently I hadn't allowed enough time for it to heal properly, and as a result, I had re-torn my MCL in September. I was able to continue working on skills and conditioning, but the pain was almost unbearable. In December, I went back for clean-up surgery and was told I couldn't resume training until February.

Perhaps my biggest mistake was comparing myself to the Shawn Johnson of 2008. I got down on myself for not performing with the same power and energy I had back then. I was especially frustrated at how long it was taking me to perform again on the floor, even though I knew my knee couldn't handle the stress of landing on the hard surface.

I get unsolicited advice all the time, but one day on a routine trip to Starbucks, I ran into a guy who told me something that completely changed my perspective. Very politely he approached me and said, "Hi, how are you? May I share something with you?"

A little warily, I agreed. We ended up talking for an hour. The gist of what he told me was this: "You'll never be what you were in 2008 because you're not the same person." Rather than thinking about how far I had to go, he suggested I think of how far I'd come.

The more I thought about it, I realized that he was right. I had a completely different body build, was now three years older, and had sustained what might have been a career-ending injury. Just a few months before, I couldn't even complete a full beam routine. Recovery wasn't fast or easy, but gradually my skills were coming back.

Though I had lost some raw power, I had gained some things as well. Until last year, I had never managed to hit a certain move, called the shaposh, on the bars. Named after Soviet gymnast Natalia Shaposhnikova, the shaposh is a difficult release move that requires you to shoot your body blindly from the low bar to the high bar. It's a skill I'd always wanted to master but never could because I was so small. The first time I nailed it, I jumped around like a giddy six-year-old.

I've also come to appreciate the wisdom my own experience brings to my training. At age fifteen or sixteen, I didn't understand all the intricacies of the sport. For instance, I didn't realize that doing a minute handstand would help me with my bar routine. When I walked into the gym, Chow would give me my assignments, and I'd just do them.

Today I understand physiology, and I understand how my body works. If I walk into the gym knowing my body simply can't work a certain way that day, Chow respects me enough to know that I'm not trying to get out of practice. I'm doing what's best for my body. We respect each other on a different level now, and it's a combined coaching partnership. Together we determine the best workout for each particular day, but I make more decisions on my own.

For five months, from February to July 2011, I was in full

training mode. Chow and I agreed that I had to take a completely different approach from the days when my goal was to perform the most difficult skills. With an injured knee, completing those skills was no longer realistic. Now my objective was to perform the cleanest, most flawless routines.

The 2011 CoverGirl Classic in Chicago would be my first competition in three years. I knew that the media and spectators had last seen me in Beijing and were likely to compare my performance to that. I had to remind myself that Chow and I had agreed this would serve as a practice run and a signal to others that I was serious about competing again. I had to accept that I did not yet have the difficult skills needed to get high scores and place in each event. My goals might have seemed simplistic: I just wanted to complete a clean routine without making any big mistakes. If I did my best on the beam and uneven bars, my two events, I would have to be satisfied.

It felt wonderful to be competing again, and the enthusiasm and support from the crowd was energizing. As I feared, though, I got a lot of flak for my performances because I wasn't yet in top shape. The highlight was competing alongside Gabby Douglas, who also trains at Chow's.

The following month I was in St. Paul for the Visa Championships. Once again, I was incredibly nervous going into the competition. This time I tied for third on beam and gave clean performances on the uneven bars and vault. A few days later I was thrilled to be named to the national team by USA Gymnastics.

In November I was off to Mexico for the Pan Am Games. Our team took the all-around gold medal; I also earned a silver medal on the bars. The last time I'd competed at the Games, I'd been the youngest team member at fifteen. This time I was the oldest American on the team, which meant I got to play the "mama" role for my teammates. Having been through it all before, I was able to offer them advice and encouragement.

Now if only I could find a way to keep myself encouraged too.

Lesson I've Learned

Be humble and patient with yourself. Take it one day at a time; you are the only person who can hold yourself back.

CHAPTER 33

JUST BELIEVE

Honor God with your body.
—1 Corinthians 6:20

"Believe in yourself." Perhaps that's the most important advice I give myself these days. When I was competing for a spot on the Olympic team in 2008, I worked incredibly hard, and success just seemed to follow. Once again, I am working incredibly hard . . . yet it doesn't come as easily as it did when I was younger, injury free, and doing gymnastics simply for the pure pleasure of it.

This time around, progress has been slower and much more painful, both physically and mentally. But I've come to realize that I'm a lot stronger than I think I am.

I get so much joy from sharing this message with people everywhere I go. I love to tell high school, middle school, and elementary students about how I found my own passion for gymnastics and how, by really putting my mind to it, my passion took me places I never dreamed of.

I'm also a stronger advocate of fitness than ever before. One key reason for making a comeback was my desire to feel athletic again, to get my body back into top shape. But I realize that many kids don't have the same love for fitness that I've always had.

That's why I jumped at the chance to partner with US Congressman Bruce Braley on the Shawn Johnson Fitness for Life Act, which he introduced in December 2011. This bill seeks to build on a unique partnership between the University of Northern Iowa and the state's Grundy Center School District. Together they incorporated technology and innovative teaching practices in physical education classes in a way that has led to higher levels of student fitness and enjoyment.

In a traditional PE class, kids might be drilled in the fundamentals of volleyball one day and then lined up and ordered to do push-ups the next. It's an approach many kids hate. And if they dread physical activity at this age, they're much less likely to be concerned about staying fit later on.

Physical education classes in the Grundy Center School District are quite different. Each day students are broken up into groups and given choices: they might work out to Dance Dance Revolution on the Wii or join in a game of dodgeball. Some might choose to go into the weight room or play baseball. Kids who absolutely hate the idea of working out on a treadmill or trying to hit a baseball in front of their classmates can choose to participate in a low-pressure activity instead.

Whatever activity they choose, all students wear heart rate monitors and know their individual target heart rate. Once they reach that heart rate, they've met their goal for the day. Of course, if they're having a blast running around while playing tag with rubber chickens, they may not want to stop. On top of that, the out-of-shape, overweight kids are likely to reach their target heart rate first. After that, they are allowed to do whatever they want. On the other hand, the track stars have to work ten times harder to reach their target heart rate since they're in better shape. This program gives small successes to those who ordinarily feel inferior for not being as in shape or as fit as the class jocks.

The real goal is to help kids discover that exercise is fun. The energy and enjoyment they get from exercise will follow them for the rest of their lives. I've been able to visit high schools that have adopted this new approach, and it's amazing to watch fourteen- and fifteen-year-olds run around the gym like they're eight, totally excited to be in gym class.

Naturally, I'm often asked if I'd like to coach gymnastics at some point. I've already had the opportunity to coach gymnastics clinics every once in a while, and I love mentoring girls and sharing my experiences with them. Yet I honestly don't see coaching as a future career for me. As much as I love gymnastics, I know too many details of what it requires of girls, both mentally and physically, to become a coach.

I'll probably do a little bit of everything in college and in my future career. I'd like to keep working with different companies, charities, and foundations as well. I can't imagine myself ever having just one job. It's not the way my mind works, and I've had to concentrate on one thing for far too long.

I want to go to college, I want to get married, and I want to have kids. And promoting fitness will always be important to me. In March 2011, I was the first gymnast to sign a sponsorship deal with Nike and was able to spend a day at the company's Oregon headquarters the following month.

Nike was interested in working with me because they believe in my story. They see my desire to earn a spot on another Olympic team as a good representation of what it means to "Just do it," the slogan that sums up what Nike is all about. Thanks to them, I'm learning more about the business of fitness. That's important to me because one of my long-term goals is to open a fitness center that makes getting in shape fun. Too often people dread going to the gym, and I want to turn that perception around. If my business eventually turned into a franchise operation, that would be a dream come true.

Whatever happens in 2012, my gymnastics career will come to an end. I still love the sport, but I'm finally at a place where I'm ready to move on. Let's face it, gymnastics doesn't last forever. In fact, it lasts a remarkably short amount of time. That's why I'm beginning to lay the groundwork for the rest of my life now.

CHAPTER 34

NO REGRETS

Dream as if you'll live forever. Live as if you'll die today.
—*James Dean*

AFTER I RETURNED from the Pan Am Games in November 2011, I had to admit that I was still dealing with a lot of residual pain from my two surgeries. To make matters worse, I often struggled with anxiety that I would tear my ACL or MCL again.

Gymnastics is one of the most dangerous sports there is, so injuries are bound to happen. Learning to be safe and to train wisely is a balance that's hard to find when you no longer have full confidence in your body. I lost that confidence when I was injured. I now understand that I'm not a machine, and I can be broken. The feelings of invincibility I once had are gone.

Looking back, I believe the pain continued because, once again, I had made my comeback a priority over rehab. For the first year after I announced my intention to make the 2012 Olympic team, I was overwhelmed with trying to multitask everything. I was trying to get my body back in shape. I was trying to get my gymnastics skill set back. I was trying to rearrange my schedule, which was full of commitments to sponsors. I felt like I was trying to take on the entire world.

Honestly, that's where my faith has been a huge help to me. My whole life I've been incredibly blessed to have parents, my cousin Tori, Coaches Chow and Li, and so many other people loving and encouraging me along the way. Yet I now know that God has always been there with me too. Not only that, but he invites me to leave everything up to him. When I try to control and handle everything myself, I get overwhelmed.

I realized that I'd been ignoring my ongoing knee problems out of fear. I was afraid that if I took time for rehab, I'd lose ground in my training—and maybe never make my comeback. Once I admitted this fear to myself, I knew I needed to take a step of faith. I had to return to rehab once more. Fortunately, my sponsor Nike wanted to support me in any way it could, and with the company's assistance, I was able to begin a six-week program at the Michael Johnson Performance Center near Dallas in early 2012.

The professionals there worked with me to strengthen my knee through intensive physical therapy and biometrics work. Just as important were my weekly meetings with my mental skills coach and with Michael Johnson, founder of the center. As a four-time Olympic gold medalist in track and field, Michael really understood the pressures I was facing in my comeback bid. Both he and my coach listened to my concerns and doubts, and they reminded me I had nothing to lose and everything to gain by seeing how far I could go this time around.

One of the hardest parts of trying for a comeback is not knowing how things will work out in the end. You know the cartoon showing a good angel sitting on one shoulder and a devil on the other? If I'm not careful, I hear that little, negative voice in my head competing with the positive one I always listened to in the past. One tells me "you can"; the other says "you can't." I'm learning the importance of staying positive on a day-to-day basis and giving it my all. I can take just one day at a time.

By mid-February I was back in West Des Moines to resume full gymnastics training and continue preparing for the Visa Championships and the Olympic Trials in June 2012. Will all the pain and stress be worth it if I don't make the Olympic team? Few things compare to the pride that comes from competing for your country with the world's best athletes. I'd be lying if I said I wouldn't love to be there, performing in the arena in London.

But in the end I have to accept that I don't have to make the team to be successful. As I learned the first time around, the judging, scoring, and placements are out of my hands anyway. I could be at the top of my game and still for some reason just not fit into the puzzle. So to me, success will mean knowing I made it as far as I possibly could, both physically and mentally. I don't yet know whether that will mean standing on the Olympic podium with a medal or traveling to London to be our team's number one cheerleader.

When I decided to return to competitive gymnastics, it was because I missed gymnastics more than I ever expected. I missed being considered an athlete and having a channel for my competitive drive. I missed having something to work for every day. I came back because I wanted to prove something to myself. I came back to get myself physically healthy and mentally happy.

In 2008, I gave 100 percent of my effort, and I'm giving 100 percent now. Back then I learned that having a winning balance doesn't always mean winning the medal; it means keeping the important things in life in balance.

When I give it everything I've got, then I've already won. I'm just thankful to know I will cross the finish line somewhere with the confidence that I couldn't have given any more. I know I can live the rest of my life with no regrets, without the nagging question "What would have happened if . . . ?" In that sense, I've got nothing to lose.

I know I have overcome so much already. All I can focus on right now is my goal for today. When I leave the gym, I look for that small success that shows my knee is a little stronger or I'm performing a skill a little better.

That's the message I want you to embrace as well. Don't allow yourself to be limited by what people say you should be doing. Follow your passion; do what seems to come most naturally to you. Follow your heart, and trust that it is pointing you in the direction you're supposed to go. Harness the energy you feel toward the activity you love, and your passion will take you to amazing places. Trust that God will walk with you through the hard times. Be grateful for the many ways he is working out all the details of your life so you can make the most of the gifts and opportunities he's given you.

God has certainly done that for me. After all, what are the odds that an energetic, risk-taking little girl from the middle of Iowa would have the opportunity to be coached by a Chinese world champion without leaving home? What are the chances that this unlikely pair would catch the eye of Bela and Martha Karolyi— and that I would eventually compete in the Olympic Games back in my coach's hometown?

If you had told me when I was a kid that I'd end up on the Olympic platform in Beijing, that I'd sign a deal with Nike, that I'd have my own Wii game, or that I'd win a popular dance competition, I wouldn't have believed it. Life can be so unexpected and startling that sometimes not knowing the future is a gift.

But there are some things that I do know.

I know that I've had the opportunity to do things others haven't even dreamed of doing.

I know that I've represented my country well in various competitions.

I know that there's honor in working hard to do something worthwhile—no matter how improbable the goal.

I know that sometimes I lose.

I know that frequently I win.

I know that either way, I'm still loved by God and my family and legions of little girls watching at home.

I know that I'm thankful for it all, win or lose.

And even though this is the last chapter of this book . . . I'm really looking forward to the next chapter of my life.

Honestly, I can't wait to see how this story unfolds.

My Heart

Grant me this eternal light.
Give me love, give me life.
Take my past and give me grace.
Walk the path to which I face.
Free my heart from this I feel.
Lift me up and help me heal.
Save me from what hurt my heart,
beat me down, and made me part,
made me fear and want to hide.
Take away the pain inside.
Give me pride and give me strength.
See the time in all its length.
Keep me close to those that care,
ones that love and want to share,
ones that help when things go wrong,
pick me up and make me strong.
Let them know what I feel inside:
burning flames that will not die.
The peace of mind and piece of heart,
forever and always they'll have a part.
Let them know they changed my life,
made me whole, and showed me the light:
re-lit the flame that burnt in here,
the passion and desire that made it clear,
then taught me how to leap and fly,

taught me love and regret,
something I will not forget.
My heart's been turned inside out,
but never once did I doubt
what it was they gave to me:
compassion, love, sincerity.

Acknowledgments

To THOSE WHO have always believed in me . . . thank you.

God: For being my greatest constant supporter, teacher, and love.

My family: For loving me and for always being there. You are my foundation and my rock to stand on. You love me for who I am, and the comfort that comes from your love and support means the world to me.

Tori: For being the sister I never had. I love you more than you could ever know. You have cheered me on since day one. Having you by my side through this whole adventure has been one of the greatest blessings of my life.

Pat: For being the best godfather, friend, and supporter! I love you, big man, and miss the old times when I would flip off your arms!

Ryan: For believing in me, supporting me, loving me, and showing me my way again. I've never learned to truly respect, love, and cherish someone so much.

The Edwards and Price families: For taking me in as one of your own. You all have taught me more than you could ever know. I love you guys, and you will forever be a part of my life!

The Oman family: For being a second family I could always count on. We've been through everything together, and I couldn't love and respect you any more than I do.

Alice and Lauren: For being the two best friends I could have ever asked for! It feels like yesterday that we were in kindergarten together. Thank you for being true and for loving me for me.

Maryah and Jessa: For being the best teammates ever. I've looked up to you girls since the first day I walked into the gym. You both have never failed to push me, love me, and continually motivate me to be better. Your heart and passion for the sport is a true blessing to see, and I will forever be grateful for what you have given me. I couldn't have made it here without you.

Taylor: For being a great friend. You've understood, listened, cared, and shared so much with me since the Olympics. You got me through one of the hardest times in my life, and I will be forever grateful for that.

Chow and Li: For giving me the opportunity to work with the best. I sincerely feel as if we have become family. Through everything, working to succeed and make you proud has been one of my biggest motivations. You are the greatest mentors an athlete could ask for.

The Michael Johnson Performance Center crew: For giving me a second chance at seeing my dreams come true. You saw the hope I had lost and turned my life back around. You gave me a new beginning and a lifelong group of friends.

Sheryl: For seeing something in me when I was thirteen years old and believing in what I had to show the world. It has been a true honor to work with you through the years, and calling you part of my family only seems natural. . . . Thank you.

My sponsors: For believing in me and supporting me so I could see my dreams come true. You have given me the chance to share my story with the world and to work with the best . . . and that's the greatest honor an athlete could ask for.

My fans: For supporting me and cheering me on. . . . I dream *big*, have fun, and follow my heart for *you*! Your loyalty means the world!

Endnotes

[1] Charlie Gibson, "ABC News Person of the Week: Shawn Johnson," *ABC World News*, September 14, 2007.

[2] USA Gymnastics, "October 17, 2007, Is 'Shawn Johnson Day' in Iowa," October 17, 2007, http://usagym.org/pages/post.html?PostID=897&prog=h.

[3] Juliet Macur, "For Some, a Silver Lining, or Even Bronze, Must Do," *New York Times*, August 17, 2008.

[4] Hy-Vee, Inc., "Shawn Johnson Makes It Official: She's Training for London Olympics in 2012," press release, May 4, 2010.

About the Author

Shawn Johnson is an Olympic gold and three-time silver medalist in women's gymnastics. She was the 2007 all-around World Champion and the 2007 and 2008 US all-around champion. Shawn won the eighth season of *Dancing with the Stars* as the youngest competitor in the show's history. She has appeared on *Oprah*, *Today*, *Late Show with David Letterman*, *The Tonight Show*, and other programs. Shawn earned ESPN's ESPY Award for Best US Female Olympian in 2009; she also won the Teen Choice Female Athlete of the Year Award in both 2009 and 2011. Visit her online at www.shawnjohnson.net.

Nancy French (collaborator) is a *New York Times* bestselling author. Her books include *A Red State of Mind: How a Catfish Queen Reject Became a Liberty Belle*; *Not Afraid of Life: My Journey So Far* (with Bristol Palin); and *Home and Away: A Story of Family in a Time of War* (with David French). She is the editor of the Faith and Family Portal at Patheos.com and can be reached at www.nancyfrench.com.

Online Discussion *guide*

TAKE *your* TYNDALE READING EXPERIENCE *to the* NEXT LEVEL

A FREE discussion guide for this book is available at bookclubhub.net, perfect for sparking conversations in your book group or for digging deeper into the text on your own.

www.bookclubhub.net

You'll also find free discussion guides for other Tyndale books, e-newsletters, e-mail devotionals, virtual book tours, and more!

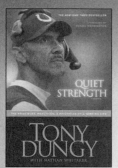
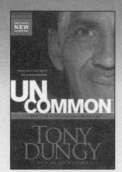
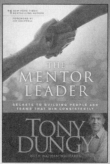

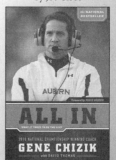